CRAZY GIBBERISH

D1166290

JAN 2013 LI

CRAZY GIBBERISH

and Other
Story Hour Stretches

(from a storyteller's bag of tricks)

by Naomi Baltuck

with whacky drawings by Doug Cushman

APPLE BOAT PRESS
an imprint of Wyatt-MacKenzie

Crazy Gibberish
And Other Story Hour Stretches
by Naomi Baltuck

ISBN: 978-1-932279-78-8

S E C O N D   E D I T I O N

Imprint information www.WyMacPublishing.com

Printed in the United States of America

APPLE BOAT PRESS

Wyatt-MacKenzie Publishing, Inc.
D E A D W O O D ,   O R E G O N

For Margie MacDonald, who gave me a gentle push
and Gene Gousie, for all the shared music and laughter

Contents

KNEE SLAPPERS, RIB TICKLERS, & TONGUE TWISTERS

WHAT EVERY GROUP LEADER SHOULD KNOW

Introduction

This book is for parents, teachers, librarians, camp counselors, scout leaders, storytellers, and anyone else who works and plays with children. I have worn all these hats, but regardless of which hat I am wearing, I bring along a matching bag—a bag full of tricks.

In that bag I keep a variety of "stretches": active stories, songs, chants, poems and nursery rhymes, jokes, riddles, tongue twisters, and games which provide an enjoyable opportunity for kids to stretch and move. Some are short, some long, some sweet, some hilarious, but all delight, incite, and invite active involvement. It is the nature of children to enjoy singing along, call and response, and the accompanying hand and foot movements.

As a mother I use them to amuse and calm my baby while driving in the car or waiting in a grocery store line. The stretches can be rowdy fun at bathtime or gifts of love to be shared at bedtime.

As a teacher I used them to add an element of spontaneous fun to the classroom, to complement a lesson, or to raise or lower the energy level of the students. If my pupils' attention began to wander, a story stretch provided a positive way of bringing it back to a central focus. The more active stretches were especially useful on rainy days, when we were restricted to indoor recess, for they provided physical activity even within the confines of our classroom. I also used them to liven up those last few minutes at the end of the day.

As a camp counselor I used to brighten up each morning with some group singing, to create a feeling of community among the campers. Sometimes we made these songs into skits for talent shows. Other times we relaxed on a hot afternoon, singing, telling stories, playing these games in the shade of a tree.

As a scout leader I used the stretches for all these reasons, but also for keeping the children "bunched" on field trips, while sitting on the beach or waiting for a bus. Some of my favorite childhood souvenirs are those songs and stretches I learned when I was a girl scout.

As a professional storyteller, I now use this material to balance my storytelling programs. A story stretch can be used to warm up an audience, close a program, add variety, or simply to help an audience "shake the ants out of its pants" in between stories. They are great fillers in case you need to adjust the length of your program or play emcee. In a worst case scenario, story stretches are excellent for crowd control because they are very engaging and don't usually require as much concentration as listening to a story does. I was once hired to tell stories at an office Christmas party that was every storyteller's worst nightmare. The kids were already sugared up, the parents in the background were all trying to shout over each others' voices (including mine). The kids who could be rounded up were holding squeaky balloons and crinkly bags of popcorn. To top it off, Santa Claus was hovering at the edge of the crowd, ready to hand out presents and more candy as soon as I was finished. I was able to hold this audience with a program consisting entirely of story stretches!

Most of the stretches included in this collection were either remembered from my childhood, or passed along to me by word of mouth. Some I learned from co-workers, others from fellow storytellers. There were several for which I simply could not find a written source, although acknowledgment of some kind is given at the back of this book. My favorite source has been the children with whom I have worked over the years.

These children's jingles are actually a unique form of folklore, passed along from child to child, generation to generation, in much the same way as jump rope rhymes, camp skits, or other indigenous children's nonsense. They are usually adapted and updated, so that each child is often quite certain that his or her peers invented these funny, often irreverent songs and games. Most often, children grow up, and these games become dim memories to their busy adult selves—only to be picked up and cherished when they become parents or, for a few years, by the next wave of children.

Whoever you are, whatever you do, if you have any contact with children, you will find your own uses for these two-minute miracles. My hope is that these will jog memories from your childhood, and perhaps even inspire you to create some story stretches for your own bag of tricks. Better yet, send me your ideas and I will try to include them in my next book!

IF YOU CAN'T CARRY A TUNE IN A BUCKET

Chants & Other Nonmusical Fun

Hi, My Name's Joe

Hi!
My name's Joe.
I got a wife, three kids. I work in the button factory.
One day the boss
Came up to me and said, "Joe,
Are you busy?"
I said, "Not."
"Turn the button with your right hand."
(turning motion with right hand)

Hi!
My name's Joe.
I got a wife, three kids. I work in the button factory.
One day the boss
Came up to me and said, "Joe,
Are you busy?"
I said, "Not."
"Turn the button with your left hand."
(turning motion with left hand)

Continue until kids are turning with right hand, left hand, right foot, left foot, head, and finally the last verse . . .

Hi!
My name's Joe.
I got a wife, three kids. I work in the button factory.

One day the boss
Came up to me and said, "Joe,
Are you busy?"
I said, "YEEESSSSS!!!!!!"
(stop all other motions and grab head with both hands)

◇

This is one of the kids' favorites. It is peppy and humorous; the words are easy and it will not take the children long to recognize the rhythm and chime in. When I introduce this stretch, I invite participation by telling the kids, "The words are easy to catch on to, so join right in." I will sometimes issue a challenge to the audience, saying, "It's pretty early in the morning for this one. It gets trickier and trickier as we go. Now we'll get to see who is really on his toes today."

Once you start each motion, continue throughout. By the end, everyone is giggling as hands, feet, and head are all going at once. Begin slowly and go faster and faster until you come to the abrupt ending.

Kindergarten through grade 6.   Time: 2 minutes

Crazy Gibberish

Teddy Bear, Teddy Bear

Teddy bear, teddy bear, turn around.
(children turn around)

Teddy bear, teddy bear, touch the ground.
(touch floor)

Teddy bear, teddy bear, show your shoe.
(lift foot and point to foot)

Teddy bear, teddy bear, that will do.
(take a bow)

Teddy bear, teddy bear, go upstairs.
(pantomime marching upstairs)

Teddy bear, teddy bear, say your prayers.
(hands together in front)

Teddy bear, teddy bear, turn around.
(turn around)

Teddy bear, teddy bear, sit back down.
(children sit down)

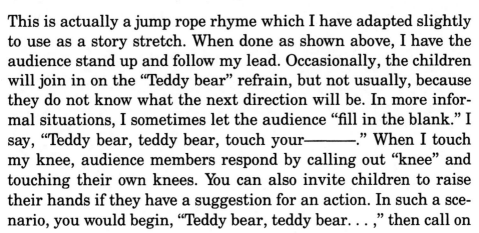

This is actually a jump rope rhyme which I have adapted slightly to use as a story stretch. When done as shown above, I have the audience stand up and follow my lead. Occasionally, the children will join in on the "Teddy bear" refrain, but not usually, because they do not know what the next direction will be. In more informal situations, I sometimes let the audience "fill in the blank." I say, "Teddy bear, teddy bear, touch your————." When I touch my knee, audience members respond by calling out "knee" and touching their own knees. You can also invite children to raise their hands if they have a suggestion for an action. In such a scenario, you would begin, "Teddy bear, teddy bear...," then call on a child with a raised hand. Listen to that child's suggestion, and then repeat it out loud for the rest of the audience while acting out the suggestion. As you make the accompanying body motions, the other audience members can follow your lead. The reason to repeat the child's suggestion is that a child's voice is usually harder to hear, especially in the back of the room. This stretch moves quickly and it would disrupt the flow of the piece to have the child come up to the front of the room to make her suggestion and/or lead the group through that one motion. Be sure to praise the child and thank her for her contribution.

Storyteller's Tip: This stretch is easily adapted to any size group and nearly any setting, from a classroom to a city bus. When space is not a concern, it can be done as shown above, by having the audience stand up beside their desks or even spread out if the space will allow. If you are concerned that some of the movements, such as turning around, are too big for your setting, you have several options. When first introducing this stretch, you can demonstrate a tidy little "teddy bear turn" with tiny turning steps and hands clasped in front, so that the children will know exactly what is expected of them. You can also do this one sitting down by simply replacing the more active movements with simple hand motions such as "touch your nose."

Preschool through grade 2.

Time: 2–5 minutes, depending upon how much action you add and how much you involve the children.

Crazy Gibberish

Oh Me, Oh My

Oh me, oh my, what'll I do?
I can't find a kangaroo to tie my ___ *(shoe)*.
But I know quite well and so do you,
I don't need a ___ *(kangaroo)* to tie my ___ *(shoe)*.

Oh me, oh my, what'll I do?
I can't find a fox to put on my ___ *(socks)*.
But I know quite well and so do you,
I don't need a ___ *(fox)* to put on my ___ *(socks)*.

Oh me, oh my, what'll I do?
I can't find a kitten to put on my ___ *(mitten)*.
But I know quite well and so do you,
I don't need a ___ *(kitten)* to put on my ___ *(mitten)*.

Oh me, oh my, what'll I do?
I can't find a goat to put on my ___ *(coat)*.
But I know quite well and so do you,
I don't need a ___ *(goat)* to put on my ___ *(coat)*.

Oh me, oh my, what'll I do?
I can't find a cat to put on my ___ *(hat)*.
But I know quite well and so do you,
I don't need a ___ *(cat)* to put on my ___ *(hat)*.

Oh me, oh my, what'll I do?
I can't find a bear to put on my ____ (hair).
But I know quite well and so do you,
I don't need a ____ (bear) to put on my ____ (hair).

Oh me, oh my, what'll I do?
I can't find a crocodile to put on my ____ (smile).
But I know quite well and so do you,
I don't need a ____ (crocodile) to put on my ____ (smile).
Because I've got YOU!

This one is most fun when the leader hams it up. Listed below are
simple motions that you can make to accompany your lines. If you
are consistent in the accompanying motions, the children will
catch on and follow along.

"Oh me, oh my, what'll I do?"	*(give shoulders a puzzled shrug)*
"I can't find a . . ."	*(shake head sadly)*
"But I know quite well,"	*(point to self and nod head in the affirmative)*
"And so do you,"	*(point to children and nod head in affirmative)*
"I don't need a . . ."	*(point to self and shake head)*
"Because I've got YOU!"	*(sweep the audience, pointing to everyone in the group)*

Let the children fill in the blanks. Pause before each missing word
and they will chime in. For each of the blanks, you can pantomime the missing word. For mitten, pantomime putting on a mit-

ten. Do the same for coat, sock, hat, etc. The children will also enjoy making up their own verses.

Storyteller's Tip: This is a gentle stretch. Its slower pace lends itself well to creative participation. You can have the children take turns coming up to the front of the room to lead the group through one whole verse.

Preschool through grade 2.

Time: 3 minutes or more, depending upon degree of group participation.

Dr. Knickerbocker

Leader: Dr. Knickerbocker, Knickerbocker,
number nine.
I just got back and I'm feeling fine.
Now let's get the rhythm of the hands.
(clap, clap)

All: Now, we've got the rhythm of the hands.
(clap, clap)

Leader: Now, let's get the rhythm of the feet.
(stomp, stomp)

All: Now, we've got the rhythm of the feet.
(stomp, stomp)

Leader: Now let's get the rhythm of the eeeeeyes.
(roll eyes and head)

All: Now, we've got the rhythm of the eeeeeyes.
(roll eyes and head)

Leader: Now let's get the rhythm of the hips,
woo, woo!
(wiggle hips, twirling index finger in air)

All: Now we've got the rhythm of the hips,
woo, woo!
(wiggle hips, twirling index finger in the air)

Leader: Now let's get the rhythm of the number nine!

All: ONE! TWO! THREE! FOUR! FIVE! SIX!
SEVEN! EIGHT! NINE!
(clap nine times as you are counting and then finish with two big stomps)

This one is done standing up. If you have the space, it is also fun to position yourselves in a circle. Invite the group to follow along. Then get a clapping rhythm going, alternately clapping your hands together and then slapping your thighs. Start the chant when you have a tempo firmly established.

After each new action, when you return to the clapping and slapping, be sure you start again with the hand clap (not the thigh slap) to get smoothly back on track.

Storyteller's Tip: This short energetic stretch is usually over too soon, for most of the kids. An offer to run through it "one more time" will probably be met with much enthusiasm. If the children know the stretch well, they can even take turns leading it.

Kindergarten through grade 6.   Time: 2 minutes

Grandma's Going to the Grocery Store

Leader: Grandma's going to the grocery store.
Group: One, two, three, four.

Leader: Grandma's going to the grocery store.
Group: One, two, three, four.

Leader: Grandma's going at a quarter past four.
Group: One, two, three, four.

Leader: Who's going?
Group: Grandma's going!

Leader: Where's she going?
Group: To the grocery store.

Leader: When's she going?
Group: At a quarter past four.

Leader: What's she gonna buy at the grocery store?
Group: One, two, three, four.

Leader: A loaf of bread,
   A bottle of milk,
   A big bag of cookies,
   And a little can of peas!

Crazy Gibberish

Group: A loaf of bread,
         A bottle of milk,
         A big bag of cookies,
         And a little can of peas!

Leader: Grandma's going to the grocery store.
Group: One, two, three, four!

This one is a call and response stretch, and it is easy enough to catch on to. When the audience is expected to answer, "one, two, three, four," hold up your fingers as a signal that they can anticipate. The other responses are self-explanatory. The only tricky one is Grandma's shopping list. For this, you can give visual cues. For a loaf of bread, hold an invisible loaf of bread in your hands; for a bottle of milk, take a swig out of an invisible milk bottle; a big bag of cookies can be shown BIG with your hands, and a little can of peas can be shown tiny with your fingers.

Storyteller's Tip: When first introducing a stretch that requires some response from an audience, until they are confident in their response, you might lead them in their part also, perhaps changing the volume of your voice and signaling with your hands and a nod of the head when it is time for them to jump in, too.

Kindergarten through grade 6.   Time: 2 minutes

My Mother Works in a Bakery

My mother works in a bakery,
Yum, yum.   *(rub stomach)*

My father works on a garbage truck,
P.U.!   *(hold nose)*
Yum, yum.   *(rub stomach)*

My sister works for the phone company.
Blah, blah!   *(hold phone to ear)*
P.U.!   *(hold nose)*
Yum, yum.   *(rub stomach)*

My brother works on a city bus.
Honk, honk.   *(honk a horn)*
Blah, blah!   *(hold phone to ear)*
P.U.!   *(hold nose)*
Yum, yum.   *(rub stomach)*

Run through the stretch with your group. If you have time, you can take suggestions from the kids for what grandma, grandpa, stepmother, stepfather, aunt, or uncle might do. Let them come up with ideas for new occupations and actions as well. Individual children can suggest an entire new verse, with an occupation and the accompanying action and sound. Or you can brainstorm as a group. For instance, you can ask the group to suggest who the next verse should be about. If a child suggests, "My dog," go with it. Now ask the group to suggest an occupation. Someone else might choose "rock star." Always repeat the suggestion aloud so that everyone can hear. Be sure to thank the child for his contribution. Continue on: "Great! Now what would a canine rock star do?" Some child will probably suggest holding an invisible guitar and strumming it. The accompanying sound could be *strum, strum* or *woof, woof.* You have now all created a brand new verse that can be used in future renditions!

If you really want to make this into a big production, each time a new verse is added, have a kid come up to the front of the room. When the group recites its cumulative list, the kids in front can go down the line, verse by verse, each repeating his part when his turn comes.

Kindergarten through grade 6.

Time: 2 minutes or more, depending upon the degree of audience participation.

TELL IT WITH ME

Audience Participation
Stories

The Teeny Weeny Bop

O nce there was a little old girl called the Teeny
Weeny Bop.
She lived all by herself and she was lonely.
One morning the Teeny Weeny Bop got up and started
sweeping her floor.
She was sweeping her floor . . .
and sweeping her floor . . .
and sweeping her floor . . .
and . . .

    She found a SILVER COIN on the floor!
    "My LUCK is MADE!" said the Teeny Weeny Bop.
    "I'll go right to town and buy myself a pet.
    Then I won't be alone anymore.
    Think I'll buy myself a fat little PIG!"
And she started off down the road.
    "TO MARKET, TO MARKET, TO BUY A FAT PIG!
    HOME AGAIN, HOME AGAIN, JIGGETY-JIG!"

She got to the town and went right to the pig farmer.
    "Mr. Pig Farmer, I have a silver coin. Could I buy a
    PIG?"
    "You sure can. Here's a fat little pig, just for you."

She put the pig under her arm and started back home.
    "I WENT TO THE MARKET, AND I BOUGHT A
    FAT PIG.
    NOW I'M COMING HOME AGAIN, JIGGETY-
    JIG!"

When she got home, she put that little pig out in her garden, and she locked the garden gate.
"You'll be safe in there, little pig."

She sat down in her chair, and she rocked, and she sang.
"I went to market, and I bought a fat pig.
Then I came home again, Jiggety-Jig."
She went to bed.
She went to sleep.
And she slept real sound.

In the morning the Teeny Weeny Bop got up and went out to check her little pig.
"Oh, NO!"
What do you think that little pig had done during the night, while she was sleeping so sound?

He had eaten up all her beans and her tomatoes.
He had rooted out all of her carrots and potatoes.
And he had made a big mud wallow right in the middle of her garden!

The Teeny Weeny Bop said,
"PIG, PIG, WHAT A MESS YOU'VE MADE!
I'M TAKING YOU TO MARKET AND I'M GOING TO TRADE!"

She thought she would trade her pig for a nice little CAT.
"TO MARKET, TO MARKET, TO BUY A FAT CAT.
HOME AGAIN, HOME AGAIN, JIGGETY-JAT."

Crazy Gibberish

She went to the cat lady.

"Ma'am, would you trade me a cat for this pig?"

"Sure. Here's a nice little cat for you."

Back home she went.

"I WENT TO MARKET, AND I BOUGHT A FAT
CAT.

NOW I'M COMING HOME AGAIN, JIGGETY-
JAT."

"I won't put this cat in the garden.

I don't want another mess.

I'll keep my cat right here . . . in the LIVING
ROOM."

She sat down in her chair, and she rocked, and she sang.

"I went to market, and I bought a fat cat.

Then I came home again, Jiggety-Jat."

She went to bed.

She went to sleep.

And she slept real sound.

In the morning, the Teeny Weeny Bop got up and
checked on her cat.

"Oh, NO!"

What do you think that cat had done while she was
sleeping so sound?

It had scratched up all the furniture.

It had ripped up the curtains.

It had knocked the lamp over and broken it.

It had made a mess of the entire living room.

She said,
"CAT, CAT, WHAT A MESS YOU'VE MADE!
I'M TAKING YOU TO MARKET AND I'M GOING
TO TRADE!"
She said,
"I think I'll get a little HAMSTER."
"TO MARKET, TO MARKET, TO BUY A FAT
HAMSTER.
HOME AGAIN, HOME AGAIN, JIGGETY-JAMS-
TER."

She went to the hamster seller.
"Hamster seller, would you trade me a hamster for
my cat?"
"Sure. Here's a fat little hamster for you."

Back home she went.
"I WENT TO MARKET, AND I BOUGHT A FAT
HAMSTER.
NOW I'M COMING HOME AGAIN, JIGGETY-
JAMSTER."

"I don't want to have any more trouble with this
pet.
I'm going to keep it safe.
I'll put it in the KITCHEN CUPBOARD!"

She sat down in her chair, she rocked, and she sang.
"I went to market, and I bought a fat hamster.
Then I came home again, Jiggety-Jamster."
She went to bed.
She went to sleep.
And she slept real sound.

In the morning the Teeny Weeny Bop got up and checked on her little pet.

"Oh, NO!"

What do you think that little hamster had done, while she was sleeping so sound?

It had eaten up all the cereal in the cupboard.
It had knocked over all the glasses and broken them.
It had chewed holes in the walls of the cupboard.
It had made a mess of everything.

She said,
> "HAMSTER, HAMSTER, WHAT A MESS YOU'VE MADE!
> I'M TAKING YOU TO MARKET AND I'M GOING TO TRADE!"

She said,
> "I think I'll buy myself a tiny pet, that won't make any trouble at all.
> I'll buy myself a fat little ANT."
> "TO MARKET, TO MARKET, TO BUY A FAT ANT.
> HOME AGAIN, HOME AGAIN, JIGGETY-JANT."

> "Ant seller, would you trade me a fat little ant for my hamster?"
> "Sure, I would. Here's your fat little ant."

Back home she went.
> "I WENT TO MARKET AND I BOUGHT A FAT ANT.
> THEN I CAME HOME AGAIN, JIGGETY-JANT."

"I'm not going to let this ant make any trouble. I'll
keep it in a safe place.
Maybe in a jar.
I know. I'll keep it in my COOKIE JAR."

She sat down in her chair, she rocked, and she sang.
"I went to market, and I bought a fat ant.
Then I came home again, Jiggety-Jant."
She went to bed.
She went to sleep.
And she slept real sound.

In the morning the Teeny Weeny Bop got up and checked
on her little pet.
"Oh, NO!"
What do you think that little ant had done while she
slept so sound?

It ate all the chocolate chips out of her cookies!
It made holes in everything.
It left nothing but a pile of crumbs and was starting to
eat those!

She said,
"ANT, ANT, WHAT A MESS YOU'VE MADE!
I'M TAKING YOU TO MARKET AND I'M GOING
TO TRADE!"

Then she said, "NO."
"I've had enough of these pets.
I don't like the ant,
I don't like the hamster,

I don't like the cat.
I think I'd rather have a fat little pig like I had in
the first place."
So she went back to the market.
"TO MARKET, TO MARKET, TO BUY A FAT PIG.
HOME AGAIN, HOME AGAIN, JIGGETY-JIG."

"Pig farmer, would you trade me a fat pig for my
ant?"
But the pig farmer would not.

"Well then, I'll trade back for a cat."

"Cat seller, would you trade me a cat for my ant?"
But the cat seller would not.

"Well, then, I'll just trade for a hamster."
But the hamster seller would not.

"Well then, I'll trade my ant back for a silver coin."

"Ant seller, would you give me a silver coin for my
ant?"
But the ant seller just laughed at her.

"I started with a silver coin.
Then I had a fat pig.
I had a fat cat.
I had a fat hamster.
Now all I have is a little ant,
and no one will trade.
I guess I've traded my luck out."

She turned the little ant loose
and she went back home, so sad.
She got her broom and started sweeping her house.
Sweeping her house . . .
and sweeping her house . . .
and sweeping her house . . .
and sweeping her house . . .
and sweeping her house . . .
and sweeping her house . . .
and . . .
   She found a SILVER COIN!

   "MY LUCK IS MADE!
   I'll go to town and buy myself a PET!
   Think I'll buy a fat little HOG!

   "TO MARKET, TO MARKET, TO BUY A FAT HOG
   HOME AGAIN, HOME AGAIN, JIGGETY-JOG."

NO MORE, NO MORE, TEENY WEENY BOP,
THIS CRAZY STORY HAS GOT TO STOP!

This near-endless story is full of possibilities for rhythm and interaction for both storyteller and audience. In the beginning, the Teeny Weeny Bop's trip to town is full of energy. Slap your thighs or snap your fingers as you chant:

   "To market, to market, to buy a fat pig.
   Home again, home again, Jiggety-Jig."

The audience will catch on quickly and join in. When she is in her chair at home, snap your fingers, slow the tempo, and chant softly.

Crazy Gibberish

While you can go with what is here, this story is ripe for improvisation. Let your audience help create the story by suggesting what animal the Teeny Weeny Bop might buy on her next trip to market. Before asking for suggestions, remind them that the animal she trades for would probably have to be smaller, because no one would want to trade a bigger animal. You can also ask them where she should keep her newest pet. Eventually someone will come up with one that will work for your story.

When you come to the line, "What do you think that little pig had done during the night, while she was sleeping so sound?," members of the audience will have lots of ideas about that. Just ask them. And finally, when the Teeny Weeny Bop returns to market to get back the pig, you can approach individuals in the audience as if they were the pig seller, the cat seller, etc., and ask if they would be willing to give a pig for your ant. When they say "No," you can even ask them why not and they will tell you that it isn't a good bargain or the ant is too small.

Be prepared to "go with the flow." If the Teeny Weeny Bop ends up trading her cat for a gerbil or a mouse or even a fish or a snake, you and your audience will be able to think of a "safe place" to keep that pet and a list of the messes it might make.

Preschool through grade 3.

Time: 11–15 minutes, depending upon the degree of audience participation.

Red Lips

There was once a girl named Jennifer who had lived in the city all her life. But the year she started middle school, her family moved to a big old house at the end of a long and lonely country lane. At first Jennifer didn't want to move, until she found out that she was going to have her own bedroom, instead of having to share with her little sister—and this bedroom was upstairs in the attic of the new house. To get to her room, she had to go up a long, dark stairway and then she had to walk down a long, dark hallway. But the room itself had been remodeled with a great big window and pretty wallpaper, and she had her very own bathroom.

At the end of moving day, Jennifer was exhausted. She had unpacked all her things, arranged her bedroom furniture, and put her posters on the walls. She fell asleep the moment her head hit the pillow.

It must have been just about midnight when Jennifer woke up in her dark, dark room. Then she heard it. A *scratch scratch scratch* on the window. "That's funny," she thought. "I'm way up on the third floor. It must be a tree branch knocking against the window pane."

She got out of bed and walked over to the window. What did she see? A hideous face pressed against the glass! It was a woman with pale white skin, long black hair, red, red lips, and long, red fingernails! And she said, "Do you know what I do with these red, red lips and these long, red fingernails?"

"No!" screamed Jennifer. She was so frightened she pulled down the window shade, jumped into her bed and pulled the covers up over her head. At last she drifted off to sleep.

In the morning, the bright sunlight streamed in through the cracks beneath the window shade and Jennifer was sure that it had all just been a bad dream. "First night jitters in the new house," she thought. She didn't even mention it to her parents or her sister. But the next night, she wasn't in any hurry to go up to bed. Finally Jennifer's mother said, "Honey, your sister has been in bed for nearly an hour. Now you go on up to bed too, or you'll never be able to get up for school tomorrow."

So Jennifer started up that long, dark stairway. *Creak, creak, creak* went the squeaky stairs. She headed down that long, dark hallway. *Creak, creak, creak*, went the squeaky floorboards. She listened outside her door. She couldn't hear anything. She opened the door (*crrrreak*), and looked all around. She didn't see anything, so she changed into her nightgown and got into bed. At last she drifted off to sleep.

It must have been just about midnight, when Jennifer woke up. Then she heard it. *Scratch, scratch, scratch* at the window. *Scratch, scratch, scratch.*

"There's nothing at the window," Jennifer told herself. "There's nothing at the window." Even so,

Jennifer got out of bed and went over to the window. What did she see? A hideous face pressed against the glass! It was a woman with pale white skin, long black hair, red, red lips and long, red fingernails. And she said, "Do you know what I do with these red, red lips and these long, red fingernails?"

"No!" screamed Jennifer, and she pulled down the window shade, jumped into bed, and pulled the covers up over her head. This time she couldn't go back to sleep. She just shivered and shook all night.

First thing in the morning, Jennifer ran downstairs and told her mother all about it. Her mother said, "I told you what would happen if you insisted upon having dill pickles with your vanilla ice cream last night. Just the thought of that gives me nightmares! Now eat your breakfast and get ready for school."

The next night, Jennifer did all her homework, helped make dinner, took out the garbage, and she even did the dishes without being asked. She did everything she could to put off going upstairs. But at last her mother said, "Honey, your sister has been in bed for nearly two hours. Now if you don't get up to bed, you'll never be able to get up for school in the morning."

Jennifer started up that long, dark stairway; it had never seemed so long and dark before (*creak, creak, creak, creak, creak, creak, creak*). She headed down that long, dark hallway; it had never seemed so long and dark before (*creak, creak, creak, creak, creak, creak, creak*). She stood listening outside her bedroom door for a long, long time. She didn't hear a sound and she knew she had to go to bed. She opened the door (*CREAK!*), jumped into her nightie, scrambled into bed, and pulled the covers up over her head all in five seconds!

Then she just shivered and shook and waited for midnight. Sure enough, it was just about midnight when she heard it. *Scratch, scratch, scratch* at the window. *Scratch, scratch, scratch.* "I'm not going to look, I'm not going to look," Jennifer told herself as she hid beneath the covers. But the *scratch, scratch, scratch* grew even louder.

"Ohhh," she moaned. "I HAVE to look!" Summoning all her courage, Jennifer whipped off her covers, marched over to the window, and there it was! That hideous face pressed against the glass! It was the woman with pale white skin, the long black hair, the red, red lips and the long, red fingernails! And she said, "Do you know what I do with these red, red lips and these long, red fingernails?"

"No!" said Jennifer.

"Well, tonight . . . I am going to SHOW you!" And the woman with the pale white skin, the long black hair, the red, red lips and the long, red fingernails took a long, red fingernail and did THIS!

(Strum index finger up and down between lips to make a silly brmm-brmm noise).

This is a story that is great for a wide age range. If you make the beginning scary, the humorous punchline will relieve the tension. Kids will want to join in on the lines that are repeated.

Miming actions will increase the fun. Here is a menu to choose from:

A hideous face pressed against the glass. Put your hands and face up to the audience as though your own face were pressed against the glass. Kids love it!

Creak, creak, creak. When creaking down the hall, have your fingers move "creepy-mouse" with each creak of the floorboards. When creaking up the stairs, start with your hands pressed together and held parallel to the floor. For each creak, move your hands, one at a time, one step higher into the air, to indicate one footstep up a stair.

Scratch, scratch, scratch. Make exaggerated motions with a hooked index finger, as though scratching on a window.

Pale white skin. Frame your own face with your hands, and look scary.

Long black hair. Gesture with your hands down from the top of your head to your waist, to indicate flowing locks.

Red, red lips. Outline your own lips with your index fingers.

Long, red fingernails. Spread your hands out wide and wiggle your fingers.

Storyteller's Tip: One way to bring the story to life is to tell it as something that actually happened to you or to a friend of yours. I often introduce this as an adventure that happened to my niece: "I always keep my eyes and ears open for a good story. You never know when you'll come across one. Last summer, when I was visiting my sister. . . ."

Like so many camp stories, this one is very adaptable. If your audience has lots of youngsters, you can play up the humor and play down the scary parts. I chose to make my protagonist a middle school student, which increased its appeal to older children.

Kindergarten through adult.   Time: 8 minutes

The Snow Queen with the Cold, Cold Heart

Once upon a time, there lived a Snow Queen with a Cold, Cold Heart (*brrrrr*). She lived far, far to the north of here in a land where the sun never shone, the snow never melted, and where the North Wind was king. The Snow Queen with the Cold, Cold Heart (*brrrrr*) had three daughters, the first of whom always had a cold in her nose (*sniffle*), the second of whom always had a cold in her chest (*cough*), and the third of whom was beautiful but sad (*ahhhhh*).

These three daughters used to love to go outside and play in the snow. They could go out in July and build a snowman, because where they lived it snowed every day of the year. Sometimes they would lie down in the snow and make snow angels. Sometimes they would build a fort and have a good old-fashioned snowball fight. Sometimes they would just go out and water their icicle garden. That is exactly what they were doing, when who should ride by (*galloping sounds*) but a Young and Handsome Prince (*aha!*)! He saw those three daughters and he promptly fell in love. Not with the Daughter with the Cold in Her Nose (*sniffle*). Not with the Daughter with the Cold in Her Chest (*cough*). He fell in love with the Daughter Who Was Beautiful But Sad (*ahhhh*).

He screeched his horse to a halt and ran into the castle of the Snow Queen with the Cold, Cold Heart (*brrrr*).

He said, "Snow Queen with the Cold, Cold Heart (*brrrr*), I wish to marry your daughter. Uh . . . NOT the Daughter with the Cold in Her Nose (*sniffle*). Not the Daughter with the Cold in Her Chest (*cough*). I want to marry the one who is, you know, Beautiful But Sad (*ahhhh*)."

"Very well," said the Snow Queen with the Cold, Cold Heart (*brrrr*). "You may marry my daughter, if she'll have you. But only on one condition. Out in forest yonder lives a Wily and Wicked Wizard (*nyah-ah-ah*). He is the one who has enchanted this land, so that the sun will never shine and the snow will never melt and one of my daughters is forever sniffling, one is forever hacking, and one is forever moping about the castle. BUT, if you take this magic potion and dash it into his face, the spell will be forever broken. Then and only then may you marry my daughter."

"I'll do it!" said the Young and Handsome Prince (*aha!*). He raced down the castle steps, leapt onto his Milk White Steed and went galloping off (*galloping noises*) toward forest yonder. He went up mountains and down through valleys. Up higher mountains and down through deeper valleys. He went through blizzards and snowstorms, through wind and through weather. At last he approached yonder enchanted forest. Who should hear him coming but the Wily and Wicked Wizard (*nyah-ah-ah*)! He ran back into his forest dwelling and came out with his magic bag of evil, dirty, nasty tricks! He reached into his bag and pulled out . . . a thunderbolt! Up came riding the Young and Handsome Prince (*aha!*) and that Wily and Wicked Wizard (*nyah-ah-ah*) let fly that thunderbolt (*whooosh!*).

It knocked him right out of the saddle, but in no time, the Young and Handsome Prince (*aha!*) was back on his feet. He whipped out that magic potion and dashed it into the face of the Wily and Wicked Wizard (*nyah-ah-ah*). And to his horror, he watched him shrink and shrivel and change into . . . a marshmallow!

It wasn't pretty, but there was nothing to be done. He picked up the marshmallow, put it into his pocket, and rode back to the castle of the Snow Queen with the Cold, Cold Heart (*brrrr*). He said, "Snow Queen with the Cold, Cold Heart (*brrrr*), I've kept my part of the bargain," and into her lap he tossed the Wily and Wicked Marshmallow. "Now you must keep your part of the bargain. If you will remember correctly, I was to marry your daughter. Uh, not the Daughter with the Cold in Her Nose (*sniffle*). Not the Daughter with the Cold in Her Chest (*cough*). You know, the Daughter Who Is Beautiful But Sad (*ahhhh*)."

"Well, as you can see," said the Snow Queen with the Cold, Cold Heart (*brrrr*), "the spell is broken. The sun is shining, the snow is starting to melt, and my daughter, while still quite beautiful, is no longer sad. And she still wants to go with you. It's all quite heart-warming, really. But do me a favor, will you? On your way out, tell my other girls to come up here for some hot chocolate. And tell them if they've been really good, I'll even put a marshmallow in it!"

And so, the Young and Handsome Prince (*aha!*) and the Daughter Who Used to Be Beautiful But Sad (*ahhhh*) rode off (*galloping sounds*) into the sunset, where they lived happily ever after, of course (*aaahhhhh!*).

Approach this action and audience participation story with a sense of fun. Ham it up and be very melodramatic in your delivery. Start out by introducing the characters one by one, explaining that everyone in your audience will get to play each part by performing the following actions and giving the proper sounds whenever each character is mentioned:

The Snow Queen with the Cold, Cold Heart: *Blow (brrrr) through your lips while holding yourself and shivering.*

The Daughter with the Cold in Her Nose: *Give a long, drawn-out sniffle while wiping your nose across your forearm in an exaggerated manner.*

The Daughter with the Cold in Her Chest: *Cover your mouth with your hand, give a couple of coughs and then a quick little groan while slumping shoulders forward.*

The Daughter Who Was Beautiful But Sad: *Assume a "far-off, dreamy look," place palms together and lift hands to one side of face, gently resting cheek on hands, while making a long breathy sigh (ahhhhh).*

The Young and Handsome Prince: *Deliver an energetic "aha!" while throwing your right fist into the air.*

Milk White Steed: *Make a galloping noise by slapping your hands on your thighs.*

Wily and Wicked Wizard: *Give a wicked cackle, "nyah-ah-ah," while rubbing your hands together and shifting your eyes from side to side.*

Kindergarten through grade 5.   Time: 10 minutes

Little Rap Riding Hood

Once upon a time there lived in the woods,
A boss little girl named Riding Hood.
I don't mean blue, I don't mean green,
I don't mean fuschia or aquamarine.

I said Red!—*(clap)*—Unh!   *(point left with right index finger)*
I said Red!—*(clap)*—Unh!   *(point right with left index finger)*
I said Red!—*(clap)*—Unh!   *(point forward and down pistol-style*
                              with both hands)

Red Riding Hood!

(Snap, two, three, four)

Granny threw out her back on her skateboard one day,
So Red took her some goodies and a tube of Ben-Gay.
"The busses aren't running and the 'vette's in the shop,
So I'll hoof it to Granny's house, clippity-clop!"

I said clop!—*(clap)*—Unh!   *(point right with left index finger)*
I said clop!—*(clap)*—Unh!   *(point left with right index finger)*
I said clop!—*(clap)*—Unh!   *(point forward and down pistol-style*
                              with both hands)

Like clippity-clop!

(Snap, two, three, four)

She was half way to Granny's a-singing a song,
When a big bad hairy wolf came along.
"Hey, hey, little girl, what's your hurry today?"
"Get lost!" said Red, and she went on her way.
But the wolf beat Red to Grandmother's pad.

He threw her in the closet (*OOOH!*)* and got in the
  bed.
When Red got there, she was really grossed out
To see a fuzz-faced Granny with a big long snout!
She had bloodshot eyes and big sharp teeth,
A big potbelly and stinky feet.
"Come closer, my dear," said the wolf in disguise.
"All the better," said Red, "for YOUR surprise."
Then Little Red jammed a Twinkie up his nose.
She stuck gum in his hair and stepped on his toes.
With one big kick, he was out on his tail.
All the way down the road, you could hear him wail.

(Snap, two, three, four)

These days wolves don't do too good,
When they pick on girls like Riding Hood.
I don't mean blue.
I don't mean green.
I don't mean fuschia or aquamarine.
I said Red!—*(clap)*—Unh!   *(point right with left index finger)*
I said Red!—*(clap)*—Unh!   *(point left with right index finger)*
I said Red!—*(clap)*—Unh!   *(point forward and down pistol-style
                            with both hands.*

Red Riding Hood! Yeah!

Snap your fingers to establish a quick, jazzy rhythm for this up-
to-date twist on a fairy tale everybody knows. Invite your audi-

---

*Give a quick squeal here, throwing up both arms in alarm, but be careful
not to lose the beat.

ence to snap their fingers right along with you. Once they recognize the rhythm of the snapping and clapping sequence, they will join in spontaneously.

In the original story of Little Red Riding Hood, both Grandmother and Little Red Riding Hood are devoured by the wolf, who is then axed to death by a woodcutter, leaving Red Riding Hood deader but wiser. More recent versions have the woodcutter racing to the rescue and cutting Grandmother and Little Red Riding Hood, no worse for the wear, out of the dead wolf's belly. While I have not cleaned all the violence out of this fairy tale, the wolf in this story is getting off fairly easy with gum in his hair and a big kick down the road. For those who question the use of any conflict or violence in fairy tales, I would highly recommend their reading Bruno Bettelheim's book, *The Uses of Enchantment*. Bettelheim explains that fairy tales with conflict give children a safe place to deal with the anger that they might be feeling. It gives them a world in which to experience danger and fear, a world in which they know that, after all is said and done, everything will work out happily ever after.

Storyteller's Tip: The timing for the clapping sequence is a little bit tricky. The clap comes AFTER the words, "I said Red!" and "I said clop!" are spoken, but the pointing of the finger occurs simultaneously with the "Unh!"

Preschool through adult.   Time: 2 minutes

Crazy Gibberish

The Squeaky Door

There was once a little boy who loved his grandmother and whose grandmother loved him. Sometimes the little boy's grandmother would say, "Sonny Boy, it's a good day for a tea party." Sometimes she would say, "Sonny Boy, it's a good day for a story." But sometimes she would say, "Sonny Boy, you're driving me crazy!"

You see, Sonny Boy loved to visit his grandmother, but he did NOT like to stay overnight at his grandmother's house. Not one bit. She lived in a great big old house. That big old house was full of big old squeaky doors. If there was one thing that Sonny Boy was afraid of, it was the sound of a squeaky door (*squeeeak!*).

One night, Sonny Boy was spending the whole night at his grandmother's house. When it was bedtime, she took him upstairs and helped him change into his pajamas. She told him a bedtime story. Then she said, "Sonny Boy, I'm going to tuck you in bed now. I'm going to kiss you goodnight. I'm going to turn out the light. Then I'm going to close the squeaky door. But you won't be scared, will you?"

Sonny Boy said, *"No, not me!"*

So Grandma tucked him in bed, gave him a big kiss (*kiss!*), turned out the light (*click!*), and she closed the squeaky door (*squeeeak!*).

OH! Sonny Boy was so scared he jumped right out of bed and said, *"WAAH!"* His grandmother came running back into the room (*footsteps*) and she said, "Sonny Boy, you're driving me crazy! I know! I'll let you sleep with the cat. Then you won't be scared, will you?"

And Sonny Boy said, "*No, not me!*"

So she went downstairs (*footsteps*), got the cat from its basket (*meow!*), carried the cat back upstairs (*more footsteps*), and tucked them in bed together. She gave them each a big kiss (*kiss!, kiss!*), turned out the light (*click!*), and she closed the squeaky door (*squeeak!*).

OH! The cat jumped out of bed and said, "*MEOW!*" Sonny Boy jumped out of bed and said, "*WAAH!*"

His grandmother came running back into the room (*footsteps*) and said, "Sonny Boy, you're driving me crazy! I know! I'll let you sleep with the dog, too. Then you won't be scared, will you?"

And Sonny Boy said, "*No, not me!*"

So she went downstairs (*footsteps*) and got the dog out of the doghouse (*woof!*), carried the dog upstairs (*more footsteps*), and tucked the dog and the cat and Sonny Boy into bed. She gave them each a big kiss (*kiss!, kiss!, kiss!*), she turned out the light (*click!*), and she closed the squeaky door (*squeeeak!*).

OH! The dog jumped out of bed and said, "*WOOF!*," the cat jumped out of bed and said, "*MEOW!*," and Sonny Boy jumped out of bed and said, "*WAAH!*"

His grandmother came running back into the room (*footsteps*) and said, "Sonny Boy, you're driving me crazy! I know! I'll let you sleep with the pig and then you won't be scared, will you?"

And Sonny Boy said, *"No, not me!"*

So she went downstairs (*footsteps*), got the pig out of the pig sty (*oink!*), carried the pig back upstairs (*more footsteps*), and tucked the pig, the dog, the cat, and Sonny Boy into bed. She gave them each a big kiss (*kiss!, kiss!, kiss!, kiss!*), turned out the light (*click!*), and closed the squeaky door (*squeeeak!*).

OH! The pig jumped out of bed and said, *"OINK!,"* the dog jumped out of bed and said, *"WOOF!,"* the cat jumped out of bed and said, *"MEOW!,"* and Sonny Boy jumped out of bed and said, *"WAAH!"*

His grandmother came running back into the room (*footsteps*) and said, "Sonny Boy, you're driving me crazy! I know! I'll let you sleep with the horse and then you won't be scared, will you?"

And Sonny Boy said, *"No, not me!"*

So she went downstairs (*footsteps*), got the horse out of the barn (*neigh!*), carried the horse upstairs (*more footsteps*), and she tucked the horse, the pig, the dog, the cat, and Sonny Boy into bed. She gave them each a big kiss (*kiss!, kiss!, kiss!, kiss!, kiss!*), and she turned out the light (*click!*). But just as she was closing the squeaky door (*squeeak!*), the horse sneezed (*achoo!*), the bed collapsed, and with a big CRASH the horse, the pig, the dog, the cat, and Sonny Boy went tumbling onto the floor.

Sonny Boy's grandmother came running back

into the room (*footsteps*). She saw the broken bed and all the animals and Sonny Boy on the floor. "That does it!" she said. "Everybody downstairs!"

Grandma marched Sonny Boy and all the animals downstairs into the kitchen where she gave them each a warm glass of milk. Then she went upstairs with her tool kit and a box of nails. She banged and she hammered and she hammered and she banged and she put the bed back together again.

But as she was putting the hammer back into her tool box, she noticed a little can with a spout on top. It was a can of OIL. Grandma chuckled to herself and said, "Now, why didn't I think of that before?" She quickly oiled the noisy hinges on that squeaky door.

Then she went downstairs and put the horse back in the barn (*NEIGH!*), she put the pig back in the pig sty (*OINK!*), she put the dog back in the doghouse (*WOOF!*), she put the cat back in her basket (*MEOW!*), and she put Sonny Boy back in his bed. "Sonny Boy, I am going to tuck you in bed, I'm going to kiss you goodnight, I'm going to turn out the light, and when I close the door, it isn't going to squeak anymore because I just oiled it, so you won't be scared, will you?"

And Sonny Boy said, "*No, not me.*"

So she tucked him in bed, she kissed him goodnight (*kiss!*), and she turned out the light (*click!*), closed the door (*silently pantomime closing the door*), and Sonny Boy fell fast asleep (*soft snoring sound*).

Now Sonny Boy LOVES to stay overnight at his

grandmother's house. They still have tea parties and story time. And even though she loves Sonny Boy very, very much, every once in a while, Grandma STILL says, *"Sonny Boy, you're driving me crazy!"*

This silly cumulative story is full of sound effects and repeated lines that encourage plenty of audience participation. When you first deliver the line, "Sonny Boy, you're driving me crazy!" be sure to draw it out humorously and the kids will be sure to join right in. They will also delight in helping you make the sound of the squeaky door, the loud smack of the goodnight kisses, and the sound of footsteps by slapping their thighs with their hands. They can look forward to helping out each time the dog barks, the cat meows, the pig oinks, when the horse sneezes, and of course, each time Sonny Boy hollers, *"WAAH!* or stoutly declares, *"No, not me!"*.

Storyteller's Tip: Each time Grandma goes downstairs, she brings back a bigger, heavier animal. Use your arms to pantomime holding your invisible burden, opening them wider each time you pick up an even bigger animal. As she gets more and more tired, have Grandma's footsteps be slower and more labored, and you can even throw in a grunt or two. By the time you get to the horse, the effect is really quite comical.

Preschool through grade 3.   Time: 13 minutes

The Tailor

In a little village there once lived a poor tailor. He had made overcoats for many people, but he had never made one for himself, though an overcoat was the one thing he wanted most. He never seemed to have enough money to buy material and set it aside for himself, without first making something to sell. But he saved and saved, bit by bit, and at last he had saved enough.

He bought the cloth and cut it carefully, so as not to waste any. He sewed up the coat, and it fit him perfectly. He was proud of that coat. He wore it even when it was the least bit cold. *He wore it and he wore it and he wore it, until at last it was all worn out.*

At least it *seemed* to be all worn out, but when he looked more closely, he could see that there was still just enough good material left to make . . . a jacket. So he cut up the coat and made a jacket. It fit just as well as the coat, and he could wear it even more often. *He wore it and he wore it and he wore it, until at last it was all worn out.*

At least it *seemed* to be worn out, but when he looked more closely, he could see that there was still just enough good material left to make . . . a vest. So he cut up the jacket and sewed a vest. He tried it on, and he looked most distinguished in that vest. He wore it every single day. *He wore it and he wore it and he wore it, until at last it was all worn out.*

At least it *seemed* to be worn out, but when he looked more closely, he could see that there was still just enough good material left to make . . . a cap. So he cut up the vest, sewed up the good pieces, and made a cap. He tried it on, and it looked just right. He wore it outdoors and in. *He wore it and he wore it and he wore it, until at last it was all worn out.*

At least it *seemed* to be worn out, but when he looked more closely, he could see that there was still just enough good material left to make . . . a button. So he cut up the cap and made a button. It was a good button. He wore it every day. *He wore it and he wore it and he wore it, until at last it was all worn out.*

At least it *seemed* to be worn out, but when he looked more closely, he could see that there was still just enough left of that button to make . . . a story. So he made a story out of that button, and I just told it to you.

This is a relatively quiet story that works well if you need to bring the energy level of an audience back down. It won't take long for the audience to catch on to the refrain and join in as you repeat the lines, "He wore it and he wore it and he wore it. . . ." and "At least it *seemed* to be worn out. . . ."

> **Storyteller's Tip:** Because of the content and conclusion of this stretch, it is also a very appropriate story to conclude a story hour with. Older audiences will enjoy the clever ending and the younger children will be enchanted as the coat gradually gets smaller and smaller. You can easily elicit further involvement from your audience. Each time you come to the line, ". . . he could see that there was still just enough good material left to make. . . ," pause, and someone in the audience will almost certainly volunteer a suggestion. If not, continue with, "What do YOU suppose?" When you get a viable answer, you can say, "That's exactly right!" and continue the story. You may stitch a new scarf, a pair of gloves, or even some underwear into the fabric of this story, but it is the idea that counts!

Preschool through grade 6, and adults.   Time: 3–6 minutes, depending upon audience participation.

SING IT HIGH, SING IT LOW

Action Songs, Musical Games, & Snappy Choruses

Who Stole the Cookie from the Cookie Jar?

All: Who stole the cookie from the cookie jar?
                Who stole the cookie from the cookie jar?
                Who stole the cookie from the cookie jar?

Leader: Jenny stole the cookie from the cookie jar!
Jenny: Who, me?
All: Yes, you!
Jenny: Couldn't be!
All: Then who?

                Who stole the cookie from the cookie jar?
                Who stole the cookie from the cookie jar?
                Who stole the cookie from the cookie jar?

Jenny: William stole the cookie from the cookie jar!
William: Who, me?
All: Yes, you!
William: Couldn't be!
All: Then who?

                Who stole the cookie . . .

Repeat rest as above

This game can be played as a lively sing-along or as a chant without actually singing. Either way, it is a fast-paced dialogue between the leader (a role which changes with each accusation), the "accused," and comments from the chorus, which is formed by the rest of the group. This is great for groups that already know one another or as a mixer for groups following brief introductions.

It is best when played sitting in a circle. Once everyone is seated, explain how the roles change with each accusation. Start out the game, and then slowly talk the group through it for the first couple of times. When you are certain that everyone understands how it works, then introduce the clapping rhythm. Get a good clapping rhythm going. Clap your hands, then slap your knees without missing a beat. The challenge of this game is to listen for your name and respond without breaking the rhythm of the beat.

Storyteller's Tip: This is a great ice-breaker; a good stretch to open a smaller group session of teaching or storytelling.

Kindergarten through grade 6.

Time: Varies, depending upon the number of participants.

Crazy Gibberish

Who Stole the Cookie from the Cookie Jar?

Ram Sam Sam

① A ram sam sam, a ram sam sam
   Guli, guli, guli, guli, guli ram sam sam.
   A ram sam sam, a ram sam sam
   Guli, guli, guli, guli, guli ram sam sam.

② Arafi, arafi,
   Guli, guli, guli, guli, guli ram sam sam.
   Arafi, arafi,
   Guli, guli, guli, guli, guli ram sam sam.

This is a popular action song with lively hand motions and an irresistible beat. For older children, you can make it more challenging by singing it as a round. The place to chime in for a two-part round is marked. "Guli" is pronounced "gooli."

ACTIONS

A ram sam sam: *Clap 3 times with emphasis on "ram sam sam".*

Guli, guli, guli, guli, guli: *Rolling motion with two hands.*

Ram sam sam: *Repeat clap 3 times.*

A ra-fi, a ra-fi: *First time: rest right elbow in left palm, point straight up, and make a small circle in the air with right index finger. Second time: rest left elbow in right palm, point straight up, and make a small circle in the air with left index finger.*

Preschool through grade 6.

Time: 2–5 minutes, depending upon how many variations you use.

Storyteller's Tip: Sing through once at a normal speed. Then sing it again faster. Then try "Super Ram Sam Sam," singing it just as fast as you can. Do a "Tiny Ram Sam Sam" using just your fingertips for the rolling motion and to clap with. Try it sitting down in a circle and using just your feet to tap out the rhythm. You and your group will be able to think up many more ways to have fun with this song. If you don't sing, it is also effective as a chant.

Action Songs, Musical Games, & Snappy Choruses

My Aunt

Leader: My aunt came back
Group: (My aunt came back)
Leader: From old Japan
Group: (From old Japan)
Leader: And brought with her
Group: (And brought with her)
Leader: A lovely fan.
Group: (A lovely fan).

(wave right hand back and forth in a fanning motion)

My aunt came back
From old Juneau
And brought with her
A fine yo-yo.

(move left hand up and down)

My aunt came back
From County Clare
And brought with her
A rocking chair.

(rock body back and forth)

My aunt came back
From old Nepal
And brought with her
A ping-pong ball.

(move head from side to side)

Crazy Gibberish

My aunt came back
From old Hong Kong
And brought with her
Some chewing gum.   *(chew in an*
exaggerated fashion)

My aunt came back
From Timbuktu
And brought with her
Some nuts like you!   *(point to audience)*

This stretch is not only an "echo" song, but a "mirror" song as well. The audience repeats each line after the leader sings it, and also mirrors the actions of the leader. Each motion, once started, is continued after the next one is added. Soon your audience will be fanning, yo-yoing, rocking, chewing, and woggling their heads all at once. The cumulative effect is hilarious!

This is a fun one for children to make up their own action verses. A frying pan from Ketchikan, a handy saw from Arkansas, a bowling ball from Montreal, a hula hoop from Guadalupe are just the tip of the iceberg of possibilities. If you do this, though, you will still want to be sure to save "Some nuts like you!" for the final verse.

Storyteller's Tip: If you don't sing, this stretch is also very effective using only the spoken voice. For the punchline, you might enjoy giving the audience the last laugh. Many in your audience will echo the last line, "Some nuts like you!" and point at the group leader. I always point to myself and repeat in mock shock, "Like ME?"

Kindergarten through grade 6   Time: 2 minutes

My Aunt

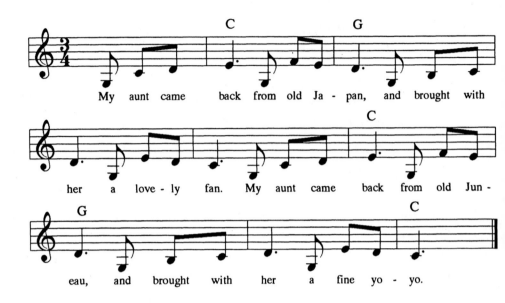

My aunt came back from old Ja - pan, and brought with her a love - ly fan. My aunt came back from old Jun - eau, and brought with her a fine yo - yo.

Crazy Gibberish

Peanut Butter

First you take the peanuts and you dig 'em,
 you dig 'em.
You dig 'em, dig 'em, dig 'em.
Then you crush 'em, you crush 'em,
You crush 'em, crush 'em, crush 'em.
And you spread 'em, you spread 'em,
You spread 'em, spread 'em, spread 'em.

Chorus: Peanut, peanut butter. Jelly!
             Peanut, peanut butter. Jelly!

Then you take the berries and you pick 'em,
 you pick 'em,
You pick 'em, pick 'em, pick 'em.
And you crush 'em, you crush 'em,
You crush 'em, crush 'em, crush 'em.
Then you spread 'em, you spread 'em,
You spread 'em, spread 'em, spread 'em.

Chorus: Peanut, peanut butter. Jelly!
             Peanut, peanut butter. Jelly!

Then you take the sandwich and you bite it,
 you bite it,
You bite it, bite it, bite it.
And you munch it, you munch it,
You munch it, munch it, munch it.

And you swallow, you swallow,
You swallow, swallow, swallow.

Chorus: Peanut, peanut butter. Jelly!
Peanut, peanut butter. Jelly!

The verses of this lively "rhythm talk" are spoken by the leader, while the chorus is sung by the children. See the music here for these few simple notes. When introducing this stretch, sing the chorus for them. Then sing it once all together. "Now you know the chorus," you can tell them, "and the rest is even easier. Just do what I do." The actions are easy; simply mime what the words describe each time the word is said. For example, "You swallow (*gulp!*), you swallow (*gulp!*) / You swallow, swallow, swallow (*gulp!*)."

ACTIONS FOR VERSES AND CHORUS

Digging: *"Dig" with an invisible shovel.*

Crushing: *"Smush" both palms together.*

Spreading: *Use the forefinger of one hand as a knife to spread P.B. or J. onto "bread"—the palm of the other hand.*

Picking berries: *Pluck berries out of the air keeping time with the rhythm.*

Take sandwich: *Hold invisible sandwich, right before your face.*

Bite it: *Move "sandwich" to mouth and chomp down.*

Munch it: *Exaggerated chewing motions.*

Swallow: *Exaggerated swallowing sound (gulp!).*

Peanut, peanut butter: *Both hands overhead and to the right, with palms gyrating in time to music.*

Jelly: *In one quick motion, thrust hands abruptly down to waist level, pointing sideways and to the left.*

Peanut Butter

First you take the pea-nuts and you dig 'em - you dig 'em - you
dig 'em, dig 'em, dig 'em. Then you crush 'em, - you crush 'em, - you
crush 'em, crush 'em, crush 'em. And you spread 'em, - you spread 'em, - you
spread 'em, spread 'em, spread 'em -. Pea-nut, pea-nut
but-ter. Jel-ly! Pea-nut, pea-nut but-ter. Jel-ly!

Storyteller's Tip: For an added surprise, when you come to the final chorus, hum the words while chewing in an exaggerated manner, as though your mouth were full of peanut butter.

Preschool through grade 3.

Time: 2 minutes

Skinnamarink

Skinnamarink a dink a dink
Skinnamarink a doo
I love you.

Skinnamarink a dink a dink
Skinnamarink a doo
I love you.

I love you in the morning
And in the afternoon.
I love you in the evening
And underneath the moon.

Skinnamarink a dink a dink
Skinnamarink a doo
I love you.

This gentle, lighthearted song is so short that you can begin by singing the whole song through, demonstrating the actions as you go. Many in your audience will begin to follow along right away. Before you begin singing the second time through, be sure to invite them to join you.

ACTIONS:

Skinnamarink a dink a dink *(cup right elbow in left hand and wave right hand)*

Skinnamarink a doo *(cup left elbow in right hand and wave left hand)*

I *(point to self)* love *(hug self)* you *(point to a member of your group)*

I love you in the morning *(put hands over head and make a circle to form the sun high in the sky)*

And in the afternoon *(gradually lower hands together to waist level)*

I love you in the evening *(lower hands further)*

And underneath the moon *(raise hands high and slightly to one side to represent a crescent moon in the sky)*

(Repeat "Skinnamarink" actions.)

Storyteller's Tip: With the final "I love you," it is fun to do a sweep of the whole group as you point your finger, so that everyone feels included. It is a very appropriate closure to a storytelling session.

Preschool through grade 3.

Time: 2 minutes

Skinnamarink

Skin - na - ma - rink a dink a dink, Skin - na - ma - rink a doo,

I love you. Skin - na - ma - rink a dink a dink,

Skin - na - ma rink a doo, I love you. I

love you in the morn - ing, and in the af - ter - noon, - I

love you in the eve - ning, and un - der - neath the moon.

Skin-na-ma-rink a dink a dink, Skin-na-ma-rink a doo, I love you.

Crazy Gibberish

Father Abraham

Father Abraham had seven sons.   *(clap! clap!)*
Seven sons had Father Abraham.
They never laughed. They never cried.   *(clap! clap!)*
All they did was go like this:
On the left.   *(wave left hand)*
On the right.   *(wave right hand)*

Father Abraham had seven sons.   *(clap! clap!)*
Seven sons had Father Abraham.
They never laughed. They never cried.   *(clap! clap!)*
All they did was go like this:
On the left.   *(hop on left foot)*
On the right.   *(hop on right foot)*
On the left.   *(wave left hand)*
On the right.   *(wave right hand)*

(And so on.)

Everyone can join in singing, as the words are simple and do not change. With each new verse, however, another action is tacked on to the end of this singing game until one's memory is really put to the test. Almost any action that can be done first on the left and then on the right (i.e., nod head, salute, swivel hips, wink eye, etc.) is appropriate. If you are having trouble keeping track of the growing number of actions, an enjoyable solution is to invite members of the audience to stand up one by one in front of the group and introduce the newest verse.

Get this stretch going smoothly by singing the first few verses and introducing very basic actions. Then explain that for the next verse, children may raise their hands to volunteer an idea for another action. Ask them to wait until you stop singing; otherwise, some will keep their hands up throughout. Also remind them ahead of time that actions must be done on both sides. Once they understand these instructions, begin again by singing the stretch through the end of the line, "All they did was go like this," and then point to a child whose hand is raised. That child can quickly come up and continue singing, "On the left, on the right," while introducing her new action. Do make sure that when the kids come up they take their places at the correct end of the line, so that the order of presentation does not get mixed up. Then, when it is time to go through the whole list of actions, you can simply go down the line of volunteers with each one singing and demonstrating the action he introduced.

Storyteller's Tip: Please do not worry if the children are actually using their right or left hands; as long as they switch sides, it doesn't really matter which hand they are using. For those who prefer, this game can be spoken as well as sung. Most importantly, always leave your audience wanting more. If you have more than eight or ten actions at the most, kids will lose interest.

Kindergarten through grade 6.

Time: 5 minutes or more, depending upon how many verses sung and the degree of audience participation.

Crazy Gibberish

Father Abraham

Fa - ther Ab - ra - ham had se - ven sons. Sev - en

sons had Fa - ther Ab - ra - ham. They nev - er

laughed. They nev - er cried. All they did was go like

1 C this. On the left. On the right.

2 C this. On the left. On the

D.C. right. On the left. On the right.

On Top of Spaghetti

(Sung to the tune of "On Top of Old Smokey")

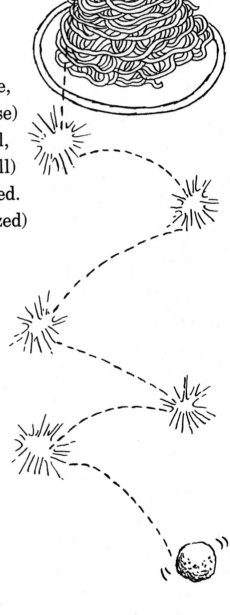

Leader: On top of spaghetti,
Group: (On top of spaghetti)
Leader: All covered with cheese,
Group: (All covered with cheese)
Leader: I lost my poor meatball,
Group: (I lost my poor meatball)
Leader: When somebody sneezed.
Group: (When somebody sneezed)

It rolled off the table
And onto the floor.
And then my poor meatball
Rolled out of the door.

It rolled into the garden
And under a bush.
And then my poor meatball
Was nothing but mush.

And early next summer
It grew into a tree,
All covered with meatballs
All ready to eat.

Crazy Gibberish

So if you eat spaghetti
All covered with cheese.
Hold onto your meatballs
And don't ever sneeze.
ACHOO!

◇

This is an echo song, with each phrase the leader sings repeated exactly by the audience. An echo song is one of the easiest types of stretch to share, because the audience does not need to be familiar with the words ahead of time. This one in particular, because of the rather sophisticated humor, is as popular with sixth graders as it is with kindergartners. This stretch is relatively low-keyed and would lend itself well to bringing down the energy level of a rowdy group.

It is a favorite among summer campers and scouting troops, where it is sometimes done with children sitting cross-legged in a circle, swaying back and forth to the music, joined hands crossed over in front. With a very large group, where sitting in a circle is not possible, the group leader can sway gently back and forth and the audience will probably do so, too.

> **Storyteller's Tip:** This song can be done in a simple and straightforward manner, but kids love it when the group leader hams this one up and sings it in a very melodramatic fashion. Also, when you come to the sneeze at the end of the song, you can either deliver the final *ACHOO!* with gusto or you can tease the audience by building up to the moment with a long drawn-out "Aaaaaah . . . aaaaaahhh . . . aaaaahhhh." When you deliver the final "*CHOOOO!*" you will probably be joined by every member in the audience. If you work with the same group over a period of time, challenge yourself to deliver up a different sneeze every time you sing it. Kids will request this song over and over again, just to see what you come up with next!

Kindergarten through grade 6.   Time: 3 minutes

Eddie C.

Chorus:
Eddie Coocha Catcha Camma Tosa Nara Tosa Noka
    Samma Camma Whacky Brown,
(WHO?)
Eddie Coocha Catcha Camma Tosa Nara Tosa Noka
    Samma Camma Whacky Brown,
Fell into the well, fell into the well, fell into the deep
    dark well.

Susie Jones,
Milking in the barn,   *(milk cow)*
Saw him fall
And ran inside to tell her mom that . . .

Chorus (repeat)

Susie's Mom,
Making crackling bread,   *(knead bread)*
Called old Joe   *(hold phone to ear)*
And told him that her Susie said that . . .

Chorus (repeat)

Then old Joe,
Laid his plow aside,   *(set plow to one side)*
Grabbed his cane   *(grab cane in one hand)*
And hobbled into town to say that . . .   *(hobble)*

Chorus (repeat)

To the well,
Everybody came.
What a shame,
It took so long to say his name that . . .

Final Chorus:
Eddie Coocha Catcha Camma Tosa Nara Tosa Noka
    Samma Camma Whacky Brown,
(WHO?)
Eddie Coocha Catcha Camma Tosa Nara Tosa Noka
    Samma Camma Whacky Brown,
DROWNED!

Sing this challenging chorus once slowly and then invite your audience to try. It is easier to learn if you break it down for them. Have them repeat after you, "Eddie Coocha Catcha Camma," then "Tosa Nara Tosa Noka," then "Samma Camma Whacky Brown." Then put them all together. Run over it a few times until your group is comfortable with it, before you add the verses. The leader sings the verses and the children join in on the chorus. To elicit the ("WHO?") response from your audience, hold your cupped hand up to your ear in an exaggerated manner.

This is a rollicking song and children love the tongue-twisty challenge. However, like so many indigenous children's chants and street rhymes, which are often laced with violence or macabre humor, this song has a rather bleak ending. Try to be sensitive to your audience. In her delightful book, *Tikki Tikki Tembo*, Arlene Mosel retells a Chinese folk tale that closely parallels the sad story of Eddie C., but the ending is much brighter. You might want to introduce the two stories together, one sung and one spoken, along with a reminder to children that they are both fictional.

Kindergarten through grade 6. Time: 5 minutes

Crazy Gibberish

Eddie C.

C-H-I-C-K-E-N

C that's the way it begins.

H that's the second letter and . . .

I I am the third and

C is the fourth letter in that word.

OK, I'm filling in.

E I'm near the end.

C-H-I-C-K-E-N, that's the way to spell chicken!

This is a bouncy, cheerful song with an irresistible beat. Before you begin this song, explain to your audience that you will be accompanying yourself with American Sign Language. American Sign Language (often called Ameslan or ASL) is used by most deaf people in the United States. Ask the kids if they can spell the word "chicken." Say the letters aloud, and then show them how to spell it with their hands, running through the letters in American Sign Language.

ASL is fascinating for children and even the sixth graders will want to try their hand at it. Don't forget to teach the kids the letters "O" and "K", because they come into the song, too. Once you have run them through it a couple of times, you can sing the song, while spelling out the letters with your hands. The kids will follow your example. This song is so short that you can then slowly run through each line of the song with the kids, holding up your hand and spelling out the word as you go. Sing it one more time all together.

Crazy Gibberish

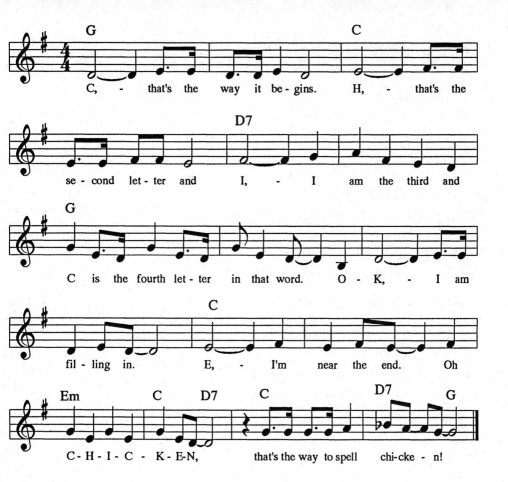

Storyteller's Tip: If you are working with a group over a period of time, once the kids all know this song, you can let them take turns coming up to the front of the room to spell out the word. It is a very simple way to let a child shine before her peers. Once the kids know all the words, you can divide the song up into parts. For instance, you can sing out the letters and let the kids sing the rest of the line or vice versa or both! For example:

Leader: **C**
Group: . . . that's the way it begins.
Leader: **H**
Group: . . . that's the second letter and . . . And so on.

Preschool through grade 6.

Time: 2 minutes.

Action Songs, Musical Games, & Snappy Choruses

The Bear in Tennis Shoes

(Sung to the tune of "Sippin' Cider Through a Straw")

Leader: The other day
Group: (The other day)
Leader: I met a bear
Group: (I met a bear)
Leader: In tennis shoes,
Group: (In tennis shoes)
Leader: A dandy pair.
Group: (A dandy pair)

All: The other day I met a bear
        In tennis shoes, a dandy pair.

He said to me,
"Why don't you run?
I see you ain't
Got any gun."

And so I ran
Away from there,
But right behind
Me was that bear.

Then up ahead,
I saw a tree.
A great big tree,
Oh, Lordy me!

Crazy Gibberish

The nearest branch
Was ten feet up.
I'd have to jump
And trust my luck.

And so I jumped
Into the air,
But I missed that branch
Away up there.

Now don't you fret,
Now don't you frown,
'Cause I caught that branch
On the way back down.

The moral of
This story is
"Don't talk to bears
In tennis shoes."

That is the end.
There ain't no more.
So what the heck
Are we singing for?

The end, the end,
The end, the end,
The end, the end,
The end, THE END!

Action Songs, Musical Games, & Snappy Choruses

This is an echo song, with the leader singing each verse phrase by phrase, echoed by the audience. Then the leader and the audience sing the verse once more all together. You can get your audience started by asking them to be your echo. Sing through the first verse, phrase by phrase. Then say, "Now we'll sing the whole verse all together." When you are through, tell them to be your echo for each phrase of each verse, but when the verse is over, they can join in and you'll sing the whole verse together. Go through that first verse one more time for practice and then keep on going.

Storyteller's Tip: There are no designated actions to go with the words of this song, but if you relax and let yourself go, there are places where you can be playful with your audience, while building the drama of this song. Take on a conversational tone, as though you are telling your audience something that really happened to you. Talk with your hands. In the first verse, when you tell them that you met a bear, puff up your chest and assume the person of a bear. When you mention his tennis shoes, point to your feet. When you relate the bear's words, speak gruffly, as a bear might speak, if he could talk. When you tell of running away, make your arms move as though you were running very quickly. Use your arms to show them just how big a tree you saw up ahead. Let them hear the tension in your voice when you tell them that you missed the branch you were grabbing for. Break the tension with a bright and cheerful delivery of the verse that begins, "Now don't you fret . . ." The children's delightful response to you will spur you on to new dramatic heights. Also, if you want to conclude a program with high energy and a rousing finale, this song, with its final verse, lends itself well to that.

Kindergarten through grade 6.   Time: 3 minutes

The Bear in Tennis Shoes

Crazy Gibberish

① Can you dig that crazy gibberish?
Can you dig it? Can you dig it?

② Can you dig that crazy gibberish?
Can you dig it? Can you dig it?

③ Hey, look, there's a chicken on the barnyard fence!
Hey, look, there's another one comin' down the road!
Maaa! Paaa! Get that son of a gun offa my tractor!

This piece is meant to be spoken in a round for two or three parts. Get everyone snapping fingers to the off beat. Practice it first all together several times. Eventually, when you feel the group is ready, you can try it as a round. Rounds, of course, are always easier if you have a co-leader to take the second part. I do not usually introduce a round in a "tell and run" situation, when there are so many easy-to-learn songs to choose from and such a limited time to work together. But when I worked with a group over a period of time, at camp, in school, and with my scout troop, we took a special pride and pleasure in singing rounds. This piece is lively enough to delight an audience, even if not performed as a round. If you are very comfortable with your group and wish to try it as a round, the place for chiming in is marked ①, ②, ③.

Storyteller's Tip: There are other places where the second and third parts could chime in to create a very interesting rhythm, but they are too difficult for most audiences to catch on to without tiresome drilling, so I use a simplified version which is easier for children who have never sung a round before. This simplified version still creates a "gibberish" that is pleasing to the ear.

Grades 3 through 6.   Time: 3 minutes

Marked for a three-part round

① Can you you dig that cra - zy gib - ber - ish? Can you

dig it? ② Can you dig it? Can you dig that cra - zy

gib - ber - ish? Can you dig it? Can you dig it? ③ Hey

look, there's a chi - cken on the barr. - yard fence. Hey

look, there's a - no - ther one com - in' down the road. Maaa!

Paaa! Get that son of a gun off - a my trac - tor!

Little Pile of Tin

Leader: I'm a little pile of tin.
Nobody knows the shape I'm in.
Got four wheels and a running board.
I'm not Chevy and I'm not Ford.

Chorus: Honk-honk, rattle, rattle, rattle,
Crash, beep, beep.
Honk-honk, rattle, rattle, rattle,
Crash, beep, beep.
Honk-honk, rattle, rattle, rattle,
Crash, beep, beep.
Honk-honk, honk-honk, honk-honk.

Leader: Romeo and Juliet,
On a balcony they met.
"Scram, you guys, I've got a date.
Shakespeare's comin' in a Ford V-8!"

Chorus (repeat)

Leader: Pepsi-Cola came to town.
Coca-Cola shot him down.
Dr. Pepper fixed him up.
Now we all drink Seven-Up.

Chorus (repeat)

Crazy Gibberish

Leader: Henry Ford was a grand old man.
Took four wheels and an old tin can.
Put 'em together and the darn thing ran.
Henry Ford was a grand old man.

Chorus (repeat)

This one, with its catchy tune and lively chorus, is a favorite of all ages. You can start out by teaching the chorus and the corresponding actions. Go through it once slowly, then faster. Now go back to the beginning and start out with the first verse. The kids will not only be delighted with the bouncy tune, but they will be looking forward to playing their part for the chorus.

ACTIONS:

Honk-honk: *Pull both ears once for each "honk"*

Rattle, rattle, rattle: *Shake head back and forth for each "rattle"*

Crash: *Gently hit chin with palm of hand*

Beep, beep: *Gently push nose like a button for each "beep"*

Honk-honk, honk-honk, honk-honk: *Again, pull both ears once for each "honk"*

Preschool through grade 6.

Time: 4 minutes

Little Pile of Tin

I'm a lit - tle pile of tin. No - bo - dy knows the
shape I'm in. Got four wheels and a run - ning board.
I'm not Che - vy and I'm not Ford. Honk honk, rat - tle rat - tle rat - tle
crash beep beep. Honk honk rat - tle rat - tle rat - tle
crash beep beep. Honk honk rat - tle rat - tle rat - tle
crash beep beep. Honk honk, honk honk, honk honk.

Crazy Gibberish

The Good Old General Store

There were ants, ants wearing rubber pants
In the store, in the store.   *(clap, clap!)*
There were ants, ants, wearing rubber pants
In the good old general store.

Chorus: My eyes are dim,   *(point to eyes)*
    I cannot see.   *(shake head)*
    I did not bring   *(point to self)*
    My specs with me.   *(make "specs" with fingers and peer through. Point to self on the word "me.")*
    I did not bring   *(point to self and shake head)*
    My specs with me.   *(make "specs" with fingers and peer through. Point to self on the word "me.")*

There were turtles, turtles, wearing fancy girdles
In the store, in the store.   *(clap, clap!)*
There were turtles, turtles, wearing fancy girdles
In the good old general store.

Chorus (repeat after each verse)

Other verses:

There was butter, butter, butter in the gutter . . .

There were snakes, snakes, snakes in the
   cornflakes . . .

There were bananas, bananas, wearing yellow
  pajamas . . .

There were eggs, eggs, with little hairy legs . . .

Kids love the whacky and fanciful imagery here. After you have
sung through all these verses, you can invite them to make up
their own. Then, one by one, sing the children's verses all together. Some of their verses will be "keepers," so be sure to write
them down for future use. The authors will beam with pride each
time their verses are sung by the group. This, by the way, makes
a great subject for a songbook for the school or classroom library,
with the children illustrating their own verses.

Preschool through grade 6.

Time: 5 minutes or more, depending
upon the number of verses sung
and the degree of audience participation.

Crazy Gibberish

The Good Old General Store

There were ants, ants, wear-ing rub-ber pants in the store, in the store. There were ants, ants, wear-ing rub-ber pants in the good old gen-eral store. My eyes are di-m, I - can-not see. I did not bring my specs with me. I did no - t bring my - y specs with me.

Little Bar of Soap

Leader: Oh, I wish I was a little bar of soap.

Group: (Bar of soap!)

Leader: Oh, I wish I was a little bar of soap.

Group: (Bar of soap!)

Leader: I'd slippy and I'd slidey over everybody's hidey.

Oh, I wish I was a little bar of soap.

Group: (Bar of soap!)

Oh, I wish I was a fishy in the sea.

(In the sea!)

Oh, I wish I was a fishy in the sea.

(In the sea!)

I'd swim around so cute without a bathing suit.

Oh, I wish I was a fishy in the sea.

(In the sea!)

Other verses:

Oh, I wish I was a little safety pin.

(Safety pin!)

And everything that busted I would hold until it rusted.

Oh, I wish I was a little mos-qui-to.
(Mos-qui-to!)
I'd go buzzy buzzy bitey under everybody's
   nightie.

Oh, I wish I was a little stri-ped skunk.
(Stri-ped skunk!)
I'd climb up in the treezes and I'd perfume all
   the breezes.

Oh, I wish I was a can of soda pop.
(Soda pop!)
I'd go down with a slurp and I'd come up with
   a burp.

The slight naughtiness of the lyrics of this call and response song
make it a favorite with younger children (some of whom actually
like to produce sound effects for the last verse!). The leader sings
out each line, and the audience echoes, with the subject of each
verse. When you first introduce this song, younger children might
be more encouraged to jump right in if you add a strong voice to
the response. If you sing both parts, indicate with your hands and
a nod of your head when the children should join in. Children do
not need to sing their response and in fact, often enjoy shouting
it. You can invite children to add their own verses, but be warned.
There are other verses of this song floating around, some of them
rather unkind ("Oh, I wish I was a little piece of glass . . .").

Storyteller's Tip: Just for fun, I like to give this song an earthy finale. In the very last
verse, instead of singing out the word "burp" I cover my mouth, widen my eyes,
and puff out my cheeks, as though stifling a burp. Kids love it.

Kindergarten through grade 5.   Time: 3 minutes

Little Bar of Soap

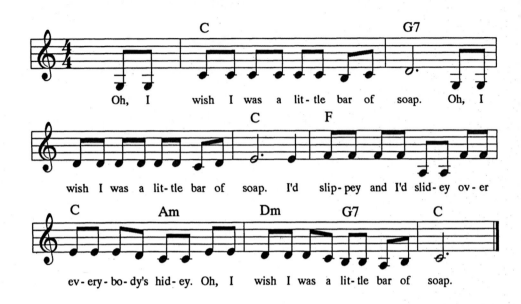

Oh, I wish I was a lit-tle bar of soap. Oh, I wish I was a lit-tle bar of soap. I'd slip-pey and I'd slid-ey ov-er ev-ery-bo-dy's hid-ey. Oh, I wish I was a lit-tle bar of soap.

Crazy Gibberish

The Princess Pat

The Princess Pat   *(Turn sideways and pose as an Ancient Egyptian)*

Lived in a tree.   *(climb an imaginary ladder)*

She sailed across   *(make waves with hand)*

The seven seas.   *(hold up seven fingers and then form a "C")*

She sailed across   *(make waves with hand)*

The Channel, too,   *(downward movement of both arms, and hold up two fingers on "two")*

And brought with her   *(swing imaginary sack over shoulder)*

A rickabamboo.   *(arms up in air, wiggle whole body downward)*

Chorus:

A rickabamboo.   *(same as before)*

Now what is that?   *(shrug shoulders)*

It's something made   *(hammer right fist with left and then left fist with right)*

By the Princess Pat.   *(same as before)*

It's red and gold   *(wiggle right hip and wrist as if twirling something)*

And purple, too.   *(wiggle left hip and wrist as if twirling something)*

That's why it's called   *(both hands to mouth as if shouting)*

A rickabamboo.   *(same as before)*

Now the Captain Jack	*(right hand salute and peer to right)*
Had a mighty fine crew.	*(left hand salute and peer to left)*
They sailed across	*(make waves with hand)*
The Channel, too.	*(same as above)*
Their ship did sink	*(hold nose, raise other hand up in air and wiggle your whole body down as if sinking)*
And so will you	*(point to audience)*
If you don't take	*(swing imaginary sack over shoulder)*
A rickabamboo.	*(same as before).*

Chorus (repeat)

Invite your audience to stand up for this one. The leader sings each line, which is repeated exactly by the audience. The leader's actions are also mirrored, making this an active and enjoyable story stretch.

Storyteller's Tip: For those who don't sing, this stretch can also be spoken, with the audience chanting back each line.

Kindergarten through grade 6.　　　　　　　　　　Time: 2 minutes

　　　　　　　　　　Crazy Gibberish

The Princess Pat

Crazy Gibberish

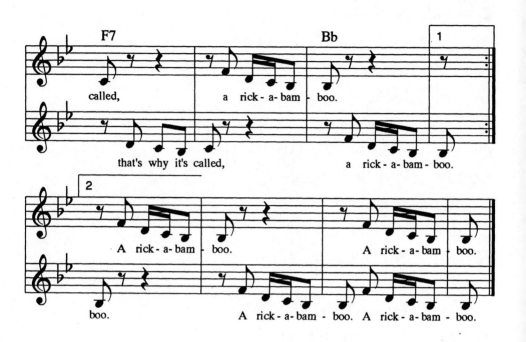

Pass It On

Leader: I wasn't there,
Group: (I wasn't there)
Leader: But somebody was.
Group: (Somebody was)
Leader: Somebody was.
Group: (Somebody was)
Leader: Somebody was.
Group: (Somebody was)
Leader: I wasn't there,
Group: (I wasn't there)
Leader: But somebody was.
Group: (Somebody was)
Leader: And they passed it along to me.
Group: (And they passed it along to me)

Continue echoes:

I won't be there,
But maybe you will.
Maybe you will.
Maybe you will.
I won't be there,
But maybe you will.
So I'll pass it along to you.

Crazy Gibberish

This gentle echo song, written by storyteller Elizabeth Ellis, seems to sum up the spirit of storytelling. With its sweet, quiet energy, it is the perfect way to close a program of stories, especially for an audience of upper primary students or older. Simply explain to your audience that you would like them to be your echo. "When I sing a line to you, you sing it right back to me." This, by the way, is a very good example of how great the possibilities are for creating your own stretches. The creator of this piece does not read music or play an instrument, and yet she has written this lovely song.

Storyteller's Tip: For an extra special touch, divide the audience into groups. If they are seated in rows, then each row can count as one group. When you come to the "pass it along" line in the last verse, have only the first row stand up and sing, "So I'll pass it along. . . ." As they sit down, the second row is standing up and singing "I'll pass it along. . . ." As soon as they finish singing the line and start to sit back down, the third row is already standing up and singing, "I'll pass it along . . ." and so on, all the way to the back of the room. If you have ever seen a crowd do "The Wave" at a football game, you can visualize how this works. The song will sweep dramatically across the audience. To keep the song-wave moving, you can travel down the side or center aisle directing with a lift of your hand to indicate to the next row when it should rise. When the last row has had its turn, you can conclude by singing the whole last line of the song, "So I'll pass it along to you." The audience will feel as though it has just been a part of a very sweet and symbolic experience.

Kindergarten through adult.   Time: 3 minutes

Pass It On

by Elizabeth Ellis

I was-n't there, but - some-bo- dy was, some- bo- dy w- as,

some - bo - dy w - as. I was - n't there, but

some - bo - dy w - as, and they passed it a - long to me.

Crazy Gibberish

We Are All the Waves of One Sea

We are all the waves of one sea.
We are all the leaves of one tree.
The time has come for all
To live as one.

We are all the flowers of one garden
And the waves of one sea
And the leaves of one tree.

This is a sweet song that is a lovely way to finish up a program. Sing it slowly and accompany yourself with American Sign Language. Invite the audience to sing along "with their hands."

Preschool through adult. 　　　　　　　　　　　　　　　Time: 2 minutes

Knee Slappers, Rib Ticklers, & Tongue Twisters

Knock, Knock

Knock, knock jokes originated in the 1920s, during the period of American history we call "Prohibition." "Speakeasys," the secret establishments that sold alcohol illegally, sprang up all over the country. But operators, always on the lookout for police, were wary of strangers. Patrons had to have some kind of code to get in. Often they would go up to the door and knock twice. The operator would ask, "Who's there?" The rest is history.

Listed below are some knock, knock jokes that could easily fit into a storytelling program. Many were chosen because they are take-offs on familiar fairy tales. Some were chosen or adapted to relate to storytelling in some way. Others are included simply because they are good for a laugh.

◇　　◇　　◇

Knock, knock.
Who's there?
Wilma.
Wilma who?
Wilma prince turn out to
　be a frog?

Knock, knock.
Who's there?
Gunnar.
Gunnar who?
Gunnar huff and puff and
　blow your house down!

Knock, knock.
Who's there?
Wolf.
Wolf who?
Wolfer goodness sake,
　what big teeth you
　have, Grandma!

Knock, knock.
Who's there?
Henny.
Henny who?
Henny Penny. And I'm
    here to tell you the sky
    is falling!

Knock, knock.
Who's there?
Otis.
Otis who?
Otis a great day for a
    story, don'tcha think?

Knock, knock.
Who's there?
Wendy.
Wendy who?
Wendy story is over, you'd
    better clap!

◇

Knock, knock.
Who's there?
Toad.
Toad who?

Toad you a story. How'd
    you like it?

Knock, knock.
Who's there?
Oswald.
Oswald who?
Oswald my gum.

Knock, knock.
Who's there?
Ether.
Ether who?
Ether bunny.

Knock, knock.
Who's there?
Estelle.
Estelle who?
Estelle more of those
    Ether bunnies!

Knock, knock.
Who's there?
Samoa.
Samoa who?
Samoa Ether bunnies.

Crazy Gibberish

Knock, knock.
Who's there?
Consumption.
Consumption who?
Consumption be done
   about all these Ether
   bunnies?

Knock, knock.
Who's there?
Hutch.
Hutch who?
Gesundheit!

◇

Knock, knock.
Who's there?
Seth.
Seth who?
Seth me! And what I seth
   goes, you hear?

◇

Knock, knock.
Who's there?
Eyes.

Eyes who?
Eyes got another "knock,
   knock" joke for you.

◇

Knock, knock.
Who's there?
Nose.
Nose who?
I nose another "knock,
   knock" joke.

◇

Knock, knock.
Who's there?
Ears.
Ears who?
Ears another "knock,
   knock" joke for you!

◇

Knock, knock.
Who's there?
Chin.
Chin who?
Chin up! I'm not going to
   tell you any more
   "knock, knock" jokes!

Storyteller's Tip: I have included several knock, knock jokes that build upon each other. You might want to use them as transitions in between several stories and conclude your program with the last joke of the series. Sharing a running joke with your audience is a great way to build rapport and, once the audience catches on, it will also enjoy anticipating the next installment.

Stories to Solve

Long before Oedipus guessed the answer to the Sphinx's riddle, the riddle was already a part of everyday life for people all over the globe. In the ancient world, many believed that a riddle had magic powers and that to guess an answer correctly was to bring good fortune. Riddles were used as a part of many sacred ceremonies and rituals. They were used by women in some Turkish tribes to test the intelligence of their suitors. They were also used to prove the greatness of leaders, as in the famous riddle war between King Solomon and the Queen of Sheba. In Hawaii, when chiefs would have a war of wits, the stakes were often very high, the loser losing also his life. Riddles have also been used to educate, to test problem-solving skills, and to provoke discussion. Even in today's world, the riddle is still a favorite form of entertainment and an important vehicle of learning. Who doesn't recall how the learning of arithmetic was made more palatable through the use of "story problems?"

Keeping in mind that people everywhere enjoy challenge, sometimes I open a storytelling program by posing a riddle and calling on the audience for their answers. It is a very effective way to get people involved from the start. I also use riddles throughout a program to vary the pace, to keep my audience alert, and to interact more directly with them.

I choose my riddles carefully. A riddle from a particular country is not only interesting in its own right, but is a good lead-in to a story from the same country. A riddle can be chosen because it complements or sheds light in some way upon the story you are about to tell. There are many clever riddles about stories and storytelling. There are many stories which are actually built around a riddle.

Some of the riddles here were chosen simply to elicit a chuckle and warm up an audience. Others are a sampling from many different lands. I selected still others because their content would easily complement a program of stories.

It is important to remember several things when you pose a riddle, whether to a large or small group. First of all, if someone makes a wrong guess to the answer, that person should not be made to feel foolish. Always be sure to say, "That's a good guess"; "Close, but not quite"; or find some other way to respond positively. Second, you must be careful not to let the questioning go on too long or your audience will grow bored or restless. When you feel that it is time to move on, you can warn them ahead of time by saying, "Let's have two more tries." If they haven't guessed by then, tell them the answer.

When I was a teacher, my students were fascinated by riddles which were posed in the form of a story. Usually one story to solve was enough for each story hour. Even so, we went through collections of African dilemma tales, George Shannon's *Stories to Solve* (he has since published *More Stories to Solve*), and even literary stories such as Frank Stockton's "The Lady or the Tiger." When I ran out of ready-made sources, I began to adapt my own. In the same way George Shannon does in both his collections of "stories to solve," you can find a story with a puzzle and a resolution that hinges on one fact, one word, or one astute observation. You can "re-arrange" the telling by skipping from the problem to the solution, and then asking your listeners how they think the story came to its conclusion. *Ooka the Wise* by I. G. Edmonds is a book of Japanese folk tales about a very wise Japanese judge who must solve many mysteries that come into his court, and he uses his wits to come to startling conclusions. This book and others like it are full of stories which work well when posed as riddles. There are many folk tales and anthologies about riddles and riddlers, such as *Hawaiian Legends of Tricksters and Riddlers* by Vivian L. Thompson, which demonstrate the importance of the riddle as a way of life in some cultures. It also shows a refreshing dependence on brains over brawn.

I hope you will use these ideas as stepping stones on your own

search for the riddles and "stories to solve" that will best complement your own repertoire of stories.

AMERICAN RIDDLES

Q. Why did Cinderella's team lose the volleyball
    game?

A. *Their coach was a pumpkin.*

Q. Why did they throw Cinderella off the baseball
    team?

A. *She kept running away from the ball.*

Q. How did Snow White break her leg?

A. *She fell off her wicked stepladder.*

Q. What did Gretel say when her stepmother left her
    in the forest?

A. *"Look, Hans, no Ma!"*

Q. Who was Sleeping Beauty's maid?

A. *Sweeping Beauty.*

Q. Which vegetables like to have a little chat with
    Jack?

A. *Jack and the beans talk.*

Q. What do Jack the Giant Killer and Alexander the
    Great have in common?

A. *The same middle name.*

Q. What is black on the inside, white on the outside, and hot?

A. *A wolf in sheep's clothing!*

Q. What's the difference between Coyote and Flea?

A. *One howls on the prairie and the other prowls on the hairy.*

Q. What's the difference between Little Goldilocks and a genealogist?

A. *A genealogist is interested in forebears, not three.*

Q. What do you get when you cross a parrot and a hyena?

A. *An animal that laughs at its own jokes!*

Q. What sits in the forest and tells long, dull stories?

A. *Smokey the Bore!*

Q. What did Noah say when the animals were finally gathered up into the ark?

A. *"Now I herd everything."*

Q. What is the tallest building in the world?

A. *The library, because it has the most stories.*

Q. Why did the skeleton go to the library?

A. *To flesh out his knowledge and bone up on things.*

Q. What's the difference between a dog and a storyteller?

A. *One has a tail that wags and the other is a wag that has tales.*

Q. What paces back and forth, back and forth on the ocean floor?
A. *A nervous wreck.*

Q. What's brown and hides in bell towers?
A. *The Lunchbag of Notre Dame.*

Q. What did the bandana say to the ten gallon hat?
A. *"You go on ahead; I'll just hang around."*

Q. What is yellow and dangerous?
A. *Shark-infested mustard!*

Q. What's worse than seeing a shark's fin in the water?
A. *Seeing his tonsils!*

Q. Why did the chicken cross the road only half way?
A. *Because she wanted to lay it on the line!*

Q. How can you eat an egg without breaking the shell?
A. *Get someone else to break it.*

Q. What does a five hundred pound canary say?
A. *"HERE KITTY, KITTY, KITTY . . ."*

Q. How can you tell if an elephant has been in your refrigerator?
A. *The footprints in the peanut butter.*

Q. How can you tell if an elephant has slept in your bed?

A. *The peanut shells under the pillow.*

Q. What's the difference between an elephant and a mailbox?

A. *You don't know? I won't ask you to mail my letters!*

Q. What do you get when you cross an elephant with a witch?

A. *I don't know, but it would take a pretty big broomstick!*

Q. Do you know why elephants never forget?

A. *No one ever tells them anything!*

TRADITIONAL RIDDLES FROM MANY LANDS

Q. How many toads' tails would it take to reach the moon?

A. *One, if it was long enough. (Scotland)*

Q. What kind of a bush does a rabbit sit under when it rains?

A. *A wet one! (Russia)*

Q. What is it people all over the world do at the same time?

A. *They grow older! (Estonia)*

Q. What grows and grows and does not die, even when you cut off its head?

A. *A fingernail! (Algeria)*

Q. Wonder, wonder, what can it be? Born in the woods, it lives on the river.

A. *A canoe. (Paraguay: Guarani)*

Q. If you want to become wise, turn me over on my back and open up my belly. What am I?

A. *A book! (Iceland)*

Q. I have a little round box, but the key that will open it is inside. What is it?

A. *An egg. (Hawaii)*

Q. When does everybody in the world speak the same language?

A. *When they are babies crying. (Siberia: Yakut)*

Q. What has no head, but plenty of tales?

A. *A big book of stories! (England)*

Q. Tie him up and he runs, but untie him and he stands still. What is it?

A. *A shoe. (Tibet)*

Q. What is no bigger than an almond, but can fill a whole room?

A. *A candle flame! (Belgium)*

Crazy Gibberish

Q. Tell me: the children are dancing, but their mother is not.

A. *The branches on a tree. (Africa: Kxatla)*

Q. The mother crawls and the children sit. What are they?

A. *Pumpkins growing from a vine. (Philippines)*

Q. What animal can swallow its own head?

A. *A turtle. (India)*

Q. I see little brothers chasing each other in the air. What are they?

A. *Sparks rising from a fire. (Alaska: Ahtna)*

Q. A great blue bowl filled with popcorn. What is it?

A. *The sky and the stars. (Mexico: Aztec)*

Q. Which animal is stronger than all the others?

A. *The skunk! (America: Comanche)*

Q. While I am held prisoner, I live. If they set me free, I die. What am I?

A. *A secret! (Spain)*

Q. Just two hairs upon her head, but she wears a flowered gown as she dances along the flower bed. What is she?

A. *A butterfly! (China)*

Q. Locked in a narrow prison, and guarded by ivory

soldiers, there is a red snake who is the mother of lies. What is it?

A. *The tongue! (Cuba)*

Q. There is a box with goods constantly being poured into, yet it is never full. What is it?

A. *The human mind. (Fiji Islands)*

Q. What walks on four legs in the morning, two legs at noon, and three legs in the evening?

A. *Man. As a baby, in the "morning" of his life, he crawls on all four legs. As a man in his prime, or the "noon time," he walks on two legs. As an old man, in the "evening" of his life, he uses a cane for his "third leg." (Greece)*

Q. Suppose there was only one tree left in the world and only one man and one axe. Then suppose the only man cut down the only tree with the only axe. If the only tree then fell upon the only man and killed him, who would be left to tell the tale?

A. *The women, of course! (Jamaica)*

Tongue Twisters and Tanglers

You might decide to use a tongue twister for some of the same reasons you would use a riddle, for it is an effective way to vary the pace or mood of a program and to have some interaction with your audience. In addition, it gives your audience a chance to be silly and laugh at itself, and it gives you all the opportunity to be playful together.

Tongue twisters, however, pose a different performance challenge. Some people might be proficient at tongue twisters and others not at all, so it is best to limit your use of them. You might supply your audience with a series of perhaps three short phrases that they can try out for a few seconds, but then move on quickly, before anyone has the time to feel actually frustrated. You might follow this up and impress the audience with your nimble-tongued telling of "Sam Short's Sparkin'," included here, or the popular "Prinderella and the Cince" by Howard L. Chace.

Begin a playful session of tongue twisting with a riddle. Ask your audience what a tongue twister is. Let them raise their hands, and call on them for their answers. Then you can say, "Well, all of you are right. It's when your tang gets all tongueled up, and have I got some tongue tanglers for *you*!"

If you are in a classroom with a chalkboard, you might want to write down the phrase you are introducing. The appearance of these short simple phrases belies the very real challenge they present. It is often helpful for the children to see the words in writing before they attempt to pronounce them.

Say each of these phrases as fast as you can, ten times in a row!

Coal oil!

Toy boat!

Greek grapes!

Lemon liniment!

(continues)

Unique New York!
Black bugs' blood!
Three grey geese!
Some shun sunshine!

This is a zither!
Sixty-six sick chickens!
Plain bun, plum bun, bun
without plum!

Now try saying these even one time through!

Rubber baby buggy bumper!
A big black bug bled black blood!
A lump of red leather, a red leather lump.
A black-backed bath brush!
A box of mixed biscuits, a mixed biscuit box!
Chop shops stock chops!
The flesh of freshly fried fish, fried fish, freshly fried!

Storyteller's Tip: If you are working with a group over a period of time, you might decide to make a tongue twister a regular feature of each story hour. On the wall of your classroom, you could keep a list of the twisters you have shared as a group. Children will start to collect them outside of story hour and bring them in to share with you. This is a good way for the children to feel they have a contribution to make. But you might want to have the child give you a preview before allowing a public performance. Unfortunately, some of the most clever tongue twisters are slightly off color. Children will undoubtedly hear them somewhere, but you probably don't want them to go home and tell their parents that they learned them from you!

Grades 3 through 6.

Time: varies

Crazy Gibberish

Glory, Glory, How Peculiar!

(Sung to the tune of "The Battle Hymn of the Republic")

One slick snake slid up the stake
And the other slick snake slid down.
One slick snake slid up the stake
And the other slick snake slid down.
One slick snake slid up the stake
And the other slick snake slid down.
One slick snake slid up the stake
And the other slick snake slid down.

Chorus:
Glory, glory, how peculiar!
Glory, glory, how peculiar!
Glory, glory, how peculiar!
That one slick snake slid up the stake
And the other slick snake slid down.

Other verses:

One pink porpoise popped over the pool
And the other pink porpoise pooped out . . .

Chorus (repeat)

One eager eagle eased under the eaves
And the other eager eagle eased east . . .

Chorus (repeat)

One rich witch's wristwatch itched
And the other rich witch's didn't . . .

Chorus (repeat)

One cute king's kite caught quite quick
And the other cute king's kite couldn't . . .

Chorus (repeat)

One sick sheik's sixth sheep was sick
And the other sick sheik's was not . . .

This song is definitely a challenge, but children, especially the upper elementary grades, delight in it. You can start out by introducing the first verse as a spoken tongue twister, having them echo it back to you one line at a time. Then put the two lines together and have them repeat the whole thing once or twice. Bring it up to tempo. Now tell them that they have actually just learned the whole first verse to a tongue twister of a song. Invite them to join in, telling them not to worry if they have not mastered the tongue twister yet, because they can practice it as they sing. Sing through the whole first verse and when you come to the chorus, you hardly need take the time to teach it. Tell them simply, "Now THIS is the easy part! Join right in on the chorus. Here's how it goes," and proceed with your "glory, how peculiars." They will chime right in. You can walk and talk them through the next verse or two, but once they understand the pattern of this song, they will happily stumble through the last few verses without practicing first.

Grades 2 through 6.   Time: 5 minutes

Sam Short's Sparkin'

by Katie L. Wheeler

(in which every word begins with "s")

Shrewd Simon Short, Smithfield's sole surviving shoemaker, sewed shoes. Seventeen summers saw Simon's small, shabby shop still standing.

Simon's spouse, Sally Short, sewed sheets, stitched shirts, stuffed sofas.

Simon's stout sturdy sons—Stephen, Samuel, Saul, Silas—sold sundries. Stephen sold silks, satins, shawls. Samuel sold saddles. Saul sold silver spoons. Silas sold Sally Short's stuffed sofas.

Simon's second son, Samuel, saw Sophia Spriggs somewhere. Sweet, sensible, smart Sophia Sophronia Spriggs. Sam soon showed strange symptoms. Surprisingly, Sam sighed sorrowfully, sang several serenades, sought Sophia's society, seldom stood selling saddles.

Sire Simon stormed, scowled severely, said, "Son Sam seems so silly singing such senseless songs."

"Softly," said sweet Sally. "Sam's smitten. Sam's spied some sweetheart."

"Smitten!" snarled Simon. "Scatterbrained simpleton! Sentimental, silly schoolboy!"

Sally sighed sadly. Summoning son Sam she spoke sympathizingly. "Sam," said she, "Sire seems singularly snappish. So, Sonny, stop strolling streets so soberly, stop singing sly serenades. Sell saddles sensibly, Sam. See Sophia Sophronia Spriggs speedily."

"So soon?" said Sam, startled.

"So soon, surely," said Sally, smilingly.

So Sam, somewhat scared, sauntered slowly, shaking stupendously. "Sophia Sophronia Spriggs . . . Sam Short's spouse . . . sounds splendid," said Sam softly.

Sam soon spied Sophia starching shirts, singing sweetly. Seeing Sam, she stopped, saluting Sam smilingly.

Sam stuttered shockingly. "S-s-splendid s-s-summer s-s-season, So-So-Sophia."

"Somewhat sultry," suggested Sophia.

"S-s-sartin," said Sam.

"Still selling saddles, Sam?" said Sophia.

"S-s-sartin," said Sam.

Silence, seventeen seconds.

"Sire shot sixteen snipe Saturday, Sam," said Sophia.

Silence, seventy-seven seconds.

"See sister Sue's sunflowers," said Sophia socially, stopping such stiff silence.

Such sprightly sauciness stimulated Sam strangely. So, swiftly speaking, Sam said, "Sue's sunflowers seem saying, 'Sophia Sophronia Spriggs, Samuel Short stroll serenely, seek some sparkling streams, sing some sweet, soul-stirring strain. . . .'"

Sophia snickered, so Sam stopped. She stood silently several seconds.

Said Sam, "Stop smiling, Sophia. Sam's seeking some sweet spouse!"

She still stood silently.

"Speak, Sophia, speak! Such silence speculates sorrow."

"Seek Sire Spriggs, Sam," said Sophia Spriggs slyly.

Sam sought Sire Spriggs.

Sire Spriggs said, "Sartin."

Grade 4 through adult.   Time: 4–5 minutes

Crazy Gibberish

WHAT EVERY GROUP
LEADER SHOULD KNOW

You don't need to read music, play an instrument, or even have a great voice to be successful in leading a group through a story stretch. If you are terrible at remembering the melodies, simplify or fake them. If you are absolutely tone deaf and couldn't carry a tune in a bucket, then forget the music and serve up that selection as a chant. This is not a singing contest: this is sharing time, creative play, building community, and making memories that will last a lifetime. Did my own Girl Scout leader have a good voice? I honestly can't remember. What I do remember is the feeling of belonging I had when we all played games and sang songs together. Thirty years later, I still remember most of those songs and games and I remember my scout leader with great affection.

The only ESSENTIAL requirement to being a successful group leader is enthusiasm. Be prepared to enjoy yourself and the children cannot help but enjoy themselves, too. Lewis Carroll once said that stories were "love gifts." Children seem to understand this. They are not judging your artistic abilities. They are not looking at you with a critical eye, so that they can laugh at your failure. They are watching you eagerly, expectantly, and they are ready to accept your "love gift" in the spirit in which it is given.

SOME RULES OF THUMB

▷ Keep your audience in mind when choosing your material. Try to have a fair idea of what would appeal to the age group you will be working with. It doesn't matter how cute "Skinnamarink" is; most sixth graders would be insulted if you tried to sing it with them. In the same vein, all the depth and meaning of "Pass It On" would be lost on the majority of preschoolers. Use your judgment, but when in doubt, take the risk and try out something new. The worst that could happen is that once will be enough and then you can move on.

▷ Whether you are working with older children or very young ones, do not patronize your audience. Even toddlers seem to understand when they are being talked down to. Be warm, be friendly, but be yourself. Treat your audience with respect and they will return it.

▷ Keep directions simple. If it takes much longer to teach than it does to sing or play, then it's probably not worth your time. Audiences will have an easier time learning stretches that are short, have simple language, and lots of repetition. The exception to this would be those songs which are intentionally challenging to learn, such as "Glory, Glory, How Peculiar!"

▷ Stay "tuned in" to your audience. Are they getting bored or restless? If so, your stretch is probably too difficult, too easy, or just too long. When this happens, finish up quickly by cutting some verses and/or choruses, or by taking a short cut to the climax of your story. Then you might bring the energy level of the group back up with a short, sure-fire favorite. It is always better to leave your audience wanting one more, than to wear out your welcome.

▷ Occasionally a new stretch will flop. Forgive yourself your failures and keep taking risks. When you discover or adapt a new stretch, you will never know for sure if it will appeal to your group until you try it out. If it works well, you will have a dynamic new stretch to add to your repertoire to use again and again. If it bombs out dreadfully, you can chalk it up to experience and waste no time worrying about it.

▷ Challenge your audience. Whether you are asking them to follow along on some crazy hand motions, try a tongue twister, or come up with some creative "fill in the blank" answers, they will enjoy rising to meet the challenge.

▷ Avoid any negative comments. If the audience is a little slow in its response, you can say, "Let's try that one more time to make sure everybody's got it." Always, always encourage them and give them positive reinforcement for their efforts: "Good job, everybody." "That was a tricky one, but you got it the very first time!" "You really had to be on your toes for that one," are just a few handy reinforcing phrases.

▷ Don't be afraid to be dramatic. Be silly, kick up your heels and have fun. Once, when I was feeling a little punchy during a summer camp song session, I led the campers in a very operatic rendition of "Over the Rainbow," using a banana for a microphone. The kids never let me forget it. That was the beginning of a new tradition: for the rest of the summer, whenever "Over the Rainbow" was requested, if a banana wasn't around, someone would place a magic marker, a spoon, or a bread stick into my hands.

INTRODUCING NEW MATERIAL

▷ When introducing a new stretch, keep instructions clear but simple. Your audience needs to know what is expected of it. One approach is to start out by singing the first verse, so that the group can hear the melody or the rhythm of a stretch. Kids will then often spontaneously join in on a snappy chorus or mirror your movements. Give them a nod of encouragement and keep on going.

Other audiences might need a more formal invitation. You can ask them to join you in many ways. Here are just a few:

"Do you remember how the chorus goes?"

"Why don't you snap your fingers here and help me get a good beat going?"

"Will you be my echo? I'll sing a line to you and you sing it right back."

"This is a tricky one. Be my mirror image; see if you can do what I do just as I'm doing it."

"You did the last one so well, I've got another one for you. It's even harder, but I know you can do it."

▷ If there is a clapping game to be learned, you can start by demonstrating slowly, letting your audience go through it a couple of times. Be sure to bring it up to speed before you all do it together as a group.

▷ Most professional entertainers, unless they are artists-in-residence, will have only one chance to meet with a particular audience. By selecting the right material, you can insure that your audience will be able to participate actively, have a roaring good time, and feel successful. Go with kid-tested favorites. An echo song or chant is perfect, because the kids have only to repeat the words you sing to them. Have a one-time-only audience do a stretch with hand and foot motions or a story where kids can provide sound effects after hearing the directions only once.

▷ If you are going to be working with the same group over the course of a summer or a school year, keep in mind that the first session is the most important one. You should still choose your favorite sure-fire stretches, so that the kids will enjoy themselves, feel successful, and look forward to the next "stretch time" together. However, you will have the enviable opportunity to build more of a rapport, a repertoire, and an ongoing sense of community with your group. With more time and opportunities to experiment, you will be able gradually to introduce more complicated songs. New verses can be added or created as the children become familiar with the stretches. You can choose just the right moment to introduce songs and stretches with more complicated verses or choruses, rounds, and tongue twisters. You will find that these stretches will provide a comfortable common ground for your group. References to or even versions of the stretches will start to pop up in their puppet shows, jokes, talent show skits, and as an inspiration for other creative projects.

▷ As you become more experienced, you will develop a better sense of what will appeal to kids, and which stretches are best suited to a particular age group. Keep in mind the fact that, while certain games and songs are recommended for certain age groups, you will probably know best what sort of material will appeal to your own group. If you have been working with a class, troop, or group of children over a period of time, you can make an educated guess.

▷ Keep lists posted on the wall. Both at camp and in the classroom, I used to introduce a new song or two at the beginning of each "stretch time," when the kids were fresh. Then I would take requests from the kids and we'd do old favorites. Each time a new song or a stretch was introduced, it was written on a big list posted on the wall. This way, kids were able to read the titles and make a request from the list. At the end of the school year or camp session, I had only to roll up my list and take it home. Then I would review it at the beginning of the next school year or summer camp session to jog my own memory as well.

▷ It is important to keep some kind of record of the stretches, because it is very easy to forget verses, melodies, or entire stretches over a period of time. If you don't read or write music, write down the verses and make a tape recording of the stretches you do not want to forget. Type up words and compile a looseleaf songbook that can be expanded upon as your repertoire grows. Audio cassettes (such as the one available for this book) also provide a "refresher course" and a stimulant.

▷ I do not recommend trying a round until and unless the group is confident of the words, rhythm, and melody. In this book, I have included only rounds which sound just as good and are as much fun to sing in one part as in a round. Start out by practicing simple, familiar rounds that everybody knows well, like "Row, Row, Row Your Boat." When they have had success in singing a round and understand how it is supposed to work, then try one of the rounds you have introduced to them.

CREATING AND ADAPTING YOUR OWN STRETCHES

▷ Neither the words nor the music to these little jingles is sacred or copyrighted, except where indicated. If you heard a stretch in passing and can't quite remember all the words, then just "fill in the blanks" with your own words. If you can't remember the tune, then make up one of your own. Most of the stretches here are old camp songs or adapted from traditional music, passed down and changed through the years. The only exception is with the copyrighted material being used by professional entertainers, in which case it is important for you to ask permission to use or adapt the material and give the author credit.

▷ You can take a traditional song that everyone will know and add some movement to it. A good example is an old favorite like "My Bonnie Lies Over the Ocean." Every time you sing a word that begins with the letter "B," for instance, have the kids stand up if they are sitting down or sit down if they are standing up. Then do it again even faster. I have seen hand motions to folk songs like "Swing Low, Sweet Chariot." Another popular folk song that most people already know, "She'll Be Coming 'Round the Mountain," can be done as a cumulative song with a long list of sounds and actions corresponding to each new verse.

▷ Personalize your songs. Instead of singing, "What will you wear, Jenny Jenkins?" or "Where, oh where is dear little Susie?," use the names of children in your group. The stretch will come alive for them as they anticipate whose name will come next. You can also use place names that will be familiar to your audience. When I sing "Turkey in the Straw," instead of "walking around the block" in Cincinnati, I change the place name in the song to Puyallup for my Washington State audiences.

▷ Need a stretch for a holiday program or a special occasion? Take a simple fingerplay or song and adapt it to suit your needs. The fingerplay, "Five Little Squirrels," can easily become "Five Little Jack O'Lanterns," "Five Little Leprechauns," or "Five Little Easter Bunnies." I have heard such songs as "Flutter, Flutter, Little Bat," sung to the tune of "Twinkle, Twinkle, Little Star."

Here's a good example of what I mean. I liked the idea of this counting fingerplay about Farmer Brown:

"Farmer Brown had five green apples hanging
  in a tree,
Farmer Brown had five green apples hanging
  in a tree,
So he plucked one apple and ate it hungrily,
Leaving four green apples hanging in a tree . . ."

I took the idea of apples disappearing from a tree, wrote a Christmas stretch about gingerbread cookies on a Christmas tree, included some places for audience participation, and added my own jazzy little melody. The result was "Five Gingerbread Cookies":

"Five gingerbread cookies on the Christmas tree,
And those five cookies looked good to me.
Along came Brother with a gleam in his eye. . . ."
(loudly stuff "cookie" into mouth and swallow)
. . . Kiss that gingerbread cookie goodbye!"

All together, with exaggerated gestures, we use our fingers to indicate that we are tiptoeing, creepy-mouse style, up to the tree and greedily looking about before we snitch another cookie from off the tree. We scarf it down, swallowing loudly, and then wave "Bye-Bye" as we "Kiss that gingerbread cookie goodbye." We sing our way down to one cookie after Sister, Daddy, and even Mommy come and snitch a cookie until . . .

"One gingerbread cookie on the Christmas tree,
Only one cookie that I could see.
Raisins for the eyes, he sure looked good . . .
(loudly stuff "cookie" into mouth and swallow)
So I gobbled him up as fast as I could.
I gobbled him up *(snap, snap)* as fast as I could!"

This is a stretch that follows a simple pattern. The melody I wrote to go with it is equally simple, but a little jazzier than some of the more common tunes for tots, and it is punctuated by silly "scarf and swallow" noises.

▷ A good sound effect is worth a thousand words. They can liven up and add humor to an otherwise ordinary stretch. Don't forget to make a place for them in your own creations.

▷ If you do sing, adding an original or a borrowed melody to a standard fingerplay will make a stretch even more interesting. A melody can help to make a story or a song easier for a child to remember. "Five Little Monkeys Jumping on the Bed," is an enjoyable fingerplay for toddlers, but after I added a simple melody, it became much more dynamic and dramatic.

▷ Jazzing up a moldy oldy is great fun, too. There is a song, "Little Cabin in the Woods," that is a cute cumulative stretch with a lot of hand motions to go with it. But I like the jazzed-up "beatnik" version of that song, "Little Cabin in the Forest Green" much better. Kids like a variation on a familiar story or song. Try your hand at a jazzed-up version of a folk or fairy tale. I wrote my own "Little Rap Riding Hood" after having such success with "The Jazzy Three Bears."

To sum it up, be creative, take a few risks, but most of all, have FUN! Let yourself go and you'll be surprised at what you can do!

If You Want to Dig Deeper: A Bibliography of Resources

One of the best places to start looking for story stretches is your own childhood. Think back to your own school, camp, or scouting days. Do you remember any of the old jump rope jingles that you used to chant with your friends on the playground? What were some of the jokes and tongue twisters that you traded with your friends in the lunchroom? Listen to what your own kids bring home from school. Try your hand at writing or adapting your very own stretches. Listed below are some resources I would recommend for those who would like to delve deeper.

BOOKS

Beall, Pamela Conn and Susan Hagen Nipp. *Wee Sing Silly Songs.* Los Angeles, Calif.: Price Stern Sloan, 1982.

Carlson, Bernice Wells. *Listen! and Help Tell the Story.* Nashville, Tenn.: Abingdon Press, 1965.

Brown, Marc. *Finger Rhymes.* New York: E. P. Dutton, 1980.

———. *Hand Rhymes.* New York: E. P. Dutton, 1985.

———. *Play Rhymes.* New York: E. P. Dutton, 1987.

Cole, Joanna and Stephanie Calmenso. *The Eentsy, Weentsy Spider: Fingerplays and Action Rhymes.* New York: Mulberry Books, 1991.

———. *Miss Mary Mack and Other Children's Street Rhymes.* New York: Morrow Junior Books, 1990.

Currie, Mary. *The Singing Sack.* London: A&C Black, 1989.

Delamar, Gloria T. *Children's Counting-Out Rhymes, Fingerplays, Jump-Rope and Ball-Bounce Chants, and Other Rhythms.* Jefferson, N.C.: McFarland, 1983.

Fowke, Edith. *Sally Go Round the Sun: 300 Songs, Rhymes, and Games of Canadian Children.* Toronto: McClelland and Steward, 1969.

Glazer, Tom. *Eye Winker, Tom Tinker, Chin Chopper.* Garden City, N.Y.: Doubleday, 1973.

Langstaff, John. *Hi! Ho! The Rattlin' Bog and Other Folk Songs for Group Singing.* New York: Harcourt, Brace & World, 1969.

MacDonald, Margaret Read. *Look Back and See: Twenty Lively Tales for Gentle Tellers.* Bronx, N.Y.: H. W. Wilson, 1991.

———. *Twenty Tellable Tales: Audience Participation Folktales for the Beginning Storyteller.* Bronx, N.Y.: H. W. Wilson, 1986.

———. *When the Lights Go Out: Twenty Scary Tales to Tell.* Bronx, N.Y.: H. W. Wilson, 1988.

Miller, Teresa. *Joining In: An Anthology of Audience Participation Stories and How to Tell Them.* Cambridge, Mass: Yellow Moon Press, 1988.

Schwartz, Alvin. *A Twister of Twists, A Tangler of Tongues.* Philadelphia: J. B. Lippincott, 1972.

Shannon, George. *Stories to Solve: Folktales from Around the World.* New York: Greenwillow Books, 1985.

———. *More Stories to Solve: Fifteen Folktales from Around the World.* New York: Greenwillow Books, 1989.

Tashjian, Virginia A. *Juba This and Juba That.* Boston: Little, Brown, 1969.

———. *With a Deep Sea Smile.* Boston: Little, Brown, 1974.

Winn, Marie. *The Fireside Book of Children's Songs.* New York: Simon and Schuster, 1966.

Wiswell, Phil. *Kids' Games: Traditional Indoor and Outdoor Activities for Children of All Ages.* New York: Doubleday, 1987.

Withers, Carl and Sula Benet. *Riddles of Many Lands.* New York: Abelard-Schuman, 1956.

RECORDINGS

Baltuck, Naomi. *Crazy Gibberish.* Audio cassette. 1993. Traveling Light, P.O. Box 836, Edmonds, Wash. 98020.

Beall, Pamela and Susan Nipp. *Wee Sing Silly Songs.* Audio cassette. 1982. Price Stern Sloan. Los Angeles, Calif.

Collins, Mitzie. *Sounds Like Fun.* Audio cassette. 1982. Sampler Records, 197 Melrose St., Rochester, N.Y. 14619.

Fink, Cathy. *Grandma Slid Down the Mountain*. Audio cassette. 1985. Rounder Records, One Camp St., Cambridge, Mass. 02140.

Harley, Bill. *Monsters in the Bathroom*. Audio cassette. 1984. Round River Records, 301 Jacob St., Seekonk, Mass. 02771.

Nagler, Eric. *Fiddle Up a Tune*. Audio cassette. 1982. Elephant Records, P.O. Box 101, Station Z, Toronto, Ontario, Canada M5N 2Z3.

———. *Improvising with Eric*. Audio cassette. 1989. Rounder Records, One Camp St., Cambridge, Mass. 02140.

Raffi. *More Singable Songs*. Audio cassette. 1977. MCA Records, 70 Universal City Plaza, University City, Calif. 91608.

———. *Singable Songs for the Very Young*. Audio cassette. 1976. MCA Records, 70 Universal City Plaza, University City, Calif. 91608.

Sharon, Lois, and Bram. *Singin' 'n' Swingin'*. Audio cassette. 1980. Elephant Records, P.O. Box 101, Station Z, Toronto, Ontario, Canada M5N 2Z3.

———. *Smorgasbord*. Audio cassette. 1979. Elephant Records, P.O. Box 101, Station Z, Toronto, Ontario, Canada M5N 2Z3.

Acknowledgments

I would like to thank Kaaren Moitoza Jacobs for her skillful transcription of the music. Thanks to my friend Margaret Read MacDonald for the push that got me going on this project and the warm encouragement that has kept me going. Thanks to my publisher, Diantha C. Thorpe, for her sensible suggestions and sound advice. Thanks to my husband, Thom, for all his patience and support and to my daughter, Eleanor, a wonderful listener, who was a baby when I began this book and is now telling ME stories! Most of all, I'd like to thank all the kids, campers, scouts, co-counselors, friends, and family with whom I have been able to share a lifelong love of fun and games.

"Hi, My Name's Joe." Traditional camp game. I cannot remember where I found this one, but storyteller Gene Gousie changed the tempo and jazzed it up. I was told by a children's librarian that its roots are in an old labor union joke that one would not want to repeat to a family audience.

"Teddy Bear, Teddy Bear." Traditional. This is a jump rope rhyme that I learned from my students and adapted slightly for use as a story stretch.

"Oh Me, Oh My." This was passed on to me by Australian story-teller Elizabeth Miller.

"Dr. Knickerbocker." Traditional. Another stretch that I learned in the early 1980s from summer day campers at Montlake Community Day Camp in Seattle, Washington.

"Grandma's Going to the Grocery Store." I was introduced to this stretch in 1991 by Sue Miller, an elementary school teacher, who uses it with her students in Seattle, Washington.

"My Mother Works in a Bakery." Traditional. One of my adult storytelling students at the University of Washington's Experimental College passed this game on to me several years ago.

"The Teeny Weeny Bop." From *Look Back and See: Twenty Lively Tales for Gentle Tellers.* © 1991 by Margaret Read MacDonald. Published by the H. W. Wilson Company. Reprinted by permission.

"Red Lips." © 1992 Naomi Baltuck. This is my version of a traditional story that has been floating around the storytelling community for some years now.

"The Snow Queen with the Cold, Cold Heart." © 1992 Naomi Baltuck. This is my adaptation of another traditional story, "The King with the Terrible Temper," which has been popular with campers and scout troops over the years.

"Little Rap Riding Hood." © 1991 Naomi Baltuck.

"The Squeaky Door." © 1992 Naomi Baltuck. There are many versions of this traditional story making the rounds in the storytelling community, but I must thank Sandra Ogren, the librarian at the Burien Public Library in Seattle, Washington, who uses it with her audiences and brought it to my attention. She based her version on a recording by singer/storytellers Rick and Judy Avery.

"The Tailor." From *Just Enough to Make a Story: A Sourcebook for Storytelling,* 3d ed., © 1992 by Nancy Schimmel. This story is based on a traditional Jewish folk song. Reprinted by permission of Nancy Schimmel.

"Who Stole the Cookie from the Cookie Jar?" Traditional. I learned this from storyteller Gene Gousie, when we were co-counselors at a summer day camp. Kaaren Moitoza Jacobs taught me the musical version.

"Ram Sam Sam." Traditional. This was taught to me by Jeanne Lusignan, a co-counselor at a ranch camp, the Bar 717, in Northern California in 1978.

"My Aunt." Traditional. I learned this in 1980 at a group sing-along at Camp Long, a recreational facility of the Seattle Parks and Recreation Department, but I never knew the name of the song leader.

"Peanut Butter." Traditional. Gene Gousie.

"Skinnamarink." Traditional. This goes back to my own elementary school years in Detroit, Michigan.

"Father Abraham." Traditional. Gene Gousie.

"On Top of Spaghetti." Traditional. This is one that I've known since my own days as a girl scout.

"Eddie C." Traditional. This was a favorite at a California summer camp, Montecito Sequoia High Sierra Camp for Girls, where I worked in 1979. It was also sung by an elementary school teacher, Kathy Knudsen, who was a camp counselor at Montlake Community Day Camp in Seattle, Washington, where we both worked.

"C-H-I-C-K-E-N." Traditional. I was introduced to this song by Gene Gousie.

"The Bear in Tennis Shoes." Traditional. Another one of those songs that I first learned as a girl scout. I also heard the late Floating Eagle Feather, a Native American storyteller, use it in a storytelling program he presented at Montlake Elementary School in Seattle, Washington in 1980.

"Crazy Gibberish." Traditional. My older sister Deborah learned this one in the Girl Scouts. Gene Gousie introduced it to the children at Montlake Community Day Camp in Seattle, Washington, where we both worked.

"Little Pile of Tin." Traditional. Gene Gousie.

"The Good Old General Store." Traditional. I have seen an Irish version of this, "The Quartermaster's Store," in several folk anthologies. In 1980, I heard the late Floating Eagle Feather, a Native American storyteller, use it to balance a program of stories he presented at Montlake Elementary School.

"Little Bar of Soap." Traditional. This was one of the songs we sang in 1979 at Montecito-Sequoia, a summer camp in Southern California.

"The Princess Pat." Haydon Lemley, one of my summer campers at Montlake Community Day Camp in Seattle, Washington, learned this stretch in the Girl Scouts in the early 1980s.

"Pass It On." © 1986 Elizabeth Ellis. I heard this Texas storyteller sing this at the National Storytelling Festival in Jonesborough, Tennessee some years ago. Reprinted by permission of the author.

"We Are All the Waves of One Sea." Traditional. Storyteller Cathryn Wellner taught me this after she learned it from storyteller Floating Eagle Feather. There are several similar versions used by the B'Hai temples here in the Pacific Northwest.

"Glory, Glory, How Peculiar!" I first heard this at a group sing at Montlake Community Day Camp in Seattle, Washington in 1980.

My friend Carol Drake remembers this one from her junior high school band practice meetings and gave me several new verses.

"Sam Short's Sparkin'" is an adaptation of "Shrewd Simon Short" from *A Twister of Twists, A Tangler of Tongues* copyright © 1972 by Alvin Schwartz. Reprinted by permission of HarperCollins Publishers. The original version of this story was written by Katie L. Wheeler in the 1890s, and may be found in the folk song section of the Library of Congress, Washington, D.C.

Crazy Gibberish

Index of Titles

Notes

Notes

Notes

Notes